Meet the American Catholic

Meet the American Catholic

Philip J. Scharper

BROADMAN PRESS
Nashville, Tennessee

TO SALLY

". . . whose spirit pure is lineal to that
which sang Magnificat."

Subject:
1. Catholic Church —history —modern.

© Copyright 1969 • Broadman Press
All rights reserved

Board binding: 422–363
Paperback: 422–364

Dewey Decimal classification: 282
Library of Congress catalog number: 69–19957
Printed in the United States of America
11.D6818

BX1389.S33 1969

Preface

What do Catholics in America really believe? How do they think and feel about their non-Catholic neighbors? What are their attitudes about some Catholic beliefs and practices that many Protestants dislike?

In a bold effort to get accurate answers to such questions, Broadman Press asked a Catholic to tell his side of the story. Philip Scharper, editor and executive for one of America's outstanding Catholic publishers, has written candidly for non-Catholic readers. Mr. Scharper is a Catholic without apology. He writes with conviction. In fact, he is capable of presenting his faith in a very attractive light. How, without listening to a well-informed Catholic, can a non-Catholic hope to understand what Catholic faith really involves?

First off, the book makes it evident that actual Catholic belief is not always what non-Catholics suppose it to be. There is great variety in Catholic views about certain questions. The belief that the Pope tells Catholics exactly what they must believe and how they must behave is not true in many important areas.

Mr. Scharper answers questions that non-Catholics ask. Part of his preparation for writing the book was consideration of a list of pointed questions submitted by non-Catholics. To pointed questions, he provides decisive answers. Often, these questions reveal misconceptions. At times, however, flat clashes of viewpoint are evident. Catholic and non-Catholic Christians hold many basic truths in common but disagree on others.

In these pages, we discover the importance that the Mass has for Catholics. In much the same way that evangelical Protestants view conversion, the Catholic sees the Mass as the way to meet and know Christ as his Saviour. The Mass, then, is far from routine.

It is on this significance of the Mass that the Catholic evaluates his Church. There is no claim that the entire Roman Church is perfect or even that its Popes are perfect. The human qualities of the Church are freely admitted. But to the Catholic, this is not the whole story. The Church is the divinely founded and sustained representative of Christ on earth—commissioned to proclaim Him and bring Him to men through the power of the Mass.

Mr. Scharper's commitment to the Church, therefore, is whole-hearted but not blind. He sees that both clergy and laity can come short of Christian ideals. Nor does he claim that it is right for them to do so. There is no pretense here that the Church is free from problems.

In quite a different sense, also, the Church emerges in these pages as a human institution. Before our eyes Catholics appear as live persons—people showing warmth, compassion, humor, courage, and determination. As non-Catholics, we have been prone to look at the worst in Catholicism and overlook the best. In order to understand Catholics, however, we have to see the best for all that it is.

Along with his affirmation of his faith and his realism in admitting some problems in Catholic life, Mr. Scharper suggests some ways that Catholic life in America may change in the future. For every reader who is curious about what is happening in Catholic life today, the book provides informative and interesting answers.

Here, then, is a refreshing picture of Catholicism as a vital faith—a faith that an intelligent man can choose and love. Readers who do not want to see that the Catholic faith possesses this kind of power may not like this book. Readers, however, who want to understand why a Catholic chooses to be a Catholic will welcome Mr. Scharper's willingness to share his faith with us.

JOSEPH F. GREEN
Editor, Specialized Books

Contents

Acknowledgments

The author wishes to thank Mr. Joseph Green of Broadman Press not only for his kind invitation to attempt this book, but for his many editorial suggestions.

The writing was done under unusual pressures of time, and could not have been done at all without the cooperation of our six children who, with silent efficiency, ran the household while my wife and I were closed off in the study. I can only hope they will feel their generosity repaid in part when they read the book they helped make possible.

To my wife, no adequate statement of thanks is possible. Much of whatever merit this book may possess is due to the qualities of her mind and heart. Every idea has been discussed with her, and has benefited as a result. In all matters a "guide, philosopher, and friend," in the case of this book she has served also as critic, editor—and typist. My fuller attempt to acknowledge my debt to her appears elsewhere in this book.

I would wish to express my appreciation also to the editors of *Ave Maria, Religious Education, The Priest* and *The Critic*. Each has kindly permitted me to use here portions of articles which had first appeared in their pages.

1
Open House

The beginning of a book is like the opening of a door through which the author invites the reader to enter. In this book I am inviting the reader to visit my spiritual home, the Roman Catholic Church. I sincerely hope that the reader will learn something of Roman Catholicism. I also promise that I shall not attempt to guide the reader quickly past those rooms within the Church about which he may long have wondered, nor shall I attempt to ignore those places where the paint is peeling or the structure in need of repair.

One further word while the reader is yet standing in the vestibule. I wish to thank him for having come, even as I thank the editors of Broadman Press for their gracious invitation to have me attempt to explain some features of Roman Catholicism to a dominantly Protestant readership. I wish that this were in fact a visit, wherein reader and author might converse instead of having the author do all the talking. I have tried to keep in mind, however, the many Protestants whom I have known, some very intimately, over many years. Their questions about Catholicism, their attitudes toward it have actually served as the material from which this book has been woven. I can only hope that I have matched the seriousness and significance of their questions with at least adequate replies.

The reader, as he moves from room to room, from chapter to chapter, will notice that the author will frequently say, "This used

to be the Catholic position, but at the moment it is changing—."
In these instances, the author will not be resorting to evasion,
nor be attempting merely to put a fair face on certain traditions
and practices within Roman Catholicism in order to recommend it
to his Protestant visitor. For the basic fact of Roman Catholicism
at the moment is precisely that it is a Church-in-Change, and
represents a massive institution of more than half a billion members, all of whom together are going through the challenging, but
often frightening, process of rapid, radical change. Some, of
course, would not hesitate to call such rapid, radical change
"revolution"; but for the average Catholic in whose name I speak
this process of change is not truly revolutionary but is seen as
the work of the Holy Spirit. It is He, in the words of a centuries-
old Christian hymn, "Who makes the arid places green, Who
straightens what has become bent, Who makes all things new."

Heaven knows, there were within the Roman Catholic Church
many fields which had grown arid, much that had become bent
and rusty, and much that was obsolescent, calling out for renewal. The amazing thing, when one looks back but ten years, is
that so few Catholics—bishops, priests, or laity—seemed to realize
that there was so much within their household of faith that was
simply old-fashioned, or in faulty working condition, or at least
covered with unsightly dust. In October, 1958, however, a short,
rotund pleasant man of peasant stock whom few people had
ever heard of, Angelo Roncalli, became Pope John XXIII.
According to news reports at the time of his election, Pope John
was chosen precisely because he was not one of the Church's outstanding prelates; he was, furthermore, of advanced age. It was
widely assumed that he would be "an interim pope," chosen to
provide the Church with a short breathing space to give her a
chance to plan what course she would take for the remainder of
the century, presumably under a younger Pope.

Pope John XXIII evidently forgot to read these press stories.
In any case, he acted like a man with much to do and little time
in which to do it. On January 25th, 1959—but few months after

his elevation to the papacy,—John XXIII announced his intention to convoke an Ecumenical Council. He told an astonished Church (and an astonished world) that he wanted the bishops and patriarchs of the worldwide Church to come together to bring about an *aggiornamento,* an up-dating, a renewal of the Catholic Church.

His closest advisors in Rome patiently told the amiable, aging Pope that it would be practically impossible to make the necessary preparations for such a worldwide Council and to bring the bishops together with a realistic agenda, unless there were years of preparation. Pope John pointed out that the Church did not have years to spend; with iron amiability, he insisted that the Council be called and be called quickly.

The rest, of course, is now history. The Second Vatican Council met from October, 1962, to December, 1965. A leading Protestant Journal, the *Christian Century,* called the Council "the most important single religious event of the twentieth century." One reason why this Protestant journal placed such high value upon the Council was because the Council which no one had expected, convoked by a Pope whom very few knew, succeeded in changing almost every aspect of the Church's life. It thereby had some effect, no matter how remote, upon every other Christian faith-community.

This Council was unlike any other in the long history of Roman Catholicism. Previous Councils had been called in times of crisis, to condemn "heresies" or thunder denunciations of "errors." The Second Vatican Council, however, instead of inveighing against heretics, caused the Church to turn with outstretched arms and newly discovered love toward men of other religions or no religion. Far from cataloging and denouncing "errors" in others, this Council took the unprecedented step of acknowledging that the Church itself had not always preserved with full integrity the treasures of Christian revelation. Previous Councils had been, in effect, almost completely European in their representation, since travel before the Jet Age made it almost impossible for the bishops of the widely scattered Church throughout the world to come to Rome in time to attend such Councils. The Second Vatican Council, however, thanks to the miracle of twentieth-century travel, saw gathered within the basilica of St. Peter's bishops and patriarchs from all over the world. They brought to the deliberations of the Council experiences, insights, and perspectives quite different from those of bishops from France, Germany, Spain or, above all, Italy. Much of the practical realism seen in the documents and pronouncements of the Second Vatican Council is due precisely to the fact that bishops from India, Japan, Africa, and South America shared with their brothers from Europe and North America the realities they had experienced in their efforts to proclaim the gospel in strange settings.

Another factor which made the Second Vatican Council unique in the Church's history lay in the fact that theologians were given a more prominent role than they had ever played before. Over the centuries, of course, theology had been given, theoretically, a very high place within the Church. Indeed, it was customary to call theology "the queen of all learning." If theology were the queen in the castle of learning, then she was queen only in the sense that Elizabeth II is the Queen of England—reigning but not allowed to rule. It would, in fact, be closer to the truth to say that theology was often found, like Cinderella, sitting amid the ashes near the hearth while her stepsisters, Church law and ethics, wore the beautiful gowns and went to the ball.

Long before the Second Vatican Council, however, the Church was blessed with a remarkable group of theologians. Their writings —in scriptural interpretation, in the theology of the Church, the Sacraments—were frequently frowned upon by high Church authorities and the theologians themselves were often in disfavor. But the great achievements of the Second Vatican Council, the profound changes which it affected, the new attitudes which it engendered among Roman Catholics, would all have been impossible if the ground had not been prepared for these sudden flowers of an unexpected spring by the work of these very theologians.

When Pope John decided to "open a window," as he put it, not a few people complained of the draught, and some became actually ill. For most people in the Church, however, a little fresh air was welcome. Until it came, it must be confessed, they hadn't noticed how stuffy the ancestral home has become.

There was one group in the Church, however, which stood by the hour before the open window, breathing deeply and stretching their limbs while the breeze blew upon their upturned, smiling faces. These were the theologians, who for some time had been making pointed remarks about the atmosphere while the rest of us thought our accustomed drowsiness was merely the aftermath of a good dinner and enforced inactivity. After all, the castle was under siege, and to open a window might invite a sniper's bullet or a Molotov cocktail. When none of these things happened, we began to look with renewed admiration at the theologians, who had told us earlier that the open window would but give sight and sound of the world the Church was called upon to serve.

As we take our tour, then, of the large and sprawling building which is Roman Catholicism, we shall have frequent occasion to note that there is scaffolding in a number of rooms, that the furniture and draperies are being rearranged in others, and that some have been completely sealed off as being almost useless. The seeming disarray of the house of Catholic faith at the moment is the direct result of the factors we have mentioned above: a portly and unpredictable Pope, John XXIII, the bishops of the worldwide Church who found themselves, quite unexpectedly, assembled for one of the most significant Councils in the Church's history, and the theologians who had labored so long and so well, most often in obscurity and very often in disfavor.

2

Myths and
Misconceptions

As we enter the house, let us pause for just a moment and look carefully at each other. You are an American Protestant, and I am a Roman Catholic. Ten years ago the mere fact that we could assign such labels to one another would have convinced us that we knew each other rather well. You "knew," that I, as a Catholic, was committed to a version of the Christian faith which was grievously distorted. Indeed, your forefathers in the faith had striven, through the Protestant Reformation, to purge the Christian Church of its aberrations and, indeed, moral turpitude. As a Catholic, I was priest-ridden, forbidden to think for myself, and thought that I could achieve salvation only by walking the tightrope of repressive and often ridiculous legislation laid down by a remote group of ecclesiastical leaders in Rome.

We Catholics, too, "knew" a great deal about Protestants. The Reformation was, in fact, the Protestant *revolt*. You were the type of person who refused to hear the authoritative teaching voice of the One True Church, preferred that each Protestant serve as his own pope, and attended church more as a place of social gathering than as the scene of worship.

Ten years ago, obviously, we dealt with each other through stereotypes. The relations between Protestant and Catholic in the United States resembled an elaborate ritual drama. Both Protestant and Catholic carried a mask before his face as they met one another in their ordinary social contacts, in business, or even when they lived together as neighbors. The irony, however, was that neither the Protestant nor the Catholic realized that there was a mask concealing his true features from the other. For the Catholic had carved the mask for the Protestant and held it before his face, even as the Protestant had carved the mask which screened the true features of his Catholic fellow citizen and neighbor from his view.

We have both come to realize, thank God, over the last ten years that we have indeed been engaged in the unblessed task of mask-making for each other. Gradually, we have begun to smash the stereotypes with which we dealt with one another. For almost the first time since the Protestant Reformation, we are beginning to see each other's face as it is, and to recognize not a foe, not a serious, sincere but misguided semi-Christian, but a brother.

The masks have not been completely removed from before our faces. This book, in effect, is intended to help the Roman Catholic remove the last vestige of the mask, to kick away the last remnant of the shattered stereotype. I can assure you that the same type of effort is going on within Roman Catholicism: a great number of Roman Catholics have taken seriously the injunction of the Second Vatican Council to study the beliefs and practices of Protestant Christians whom we now officially call, not "heretics," but our "separated brothers."

This chapter, then, will attempt to deal with certain myths and misconceptions which a significant number of Protestants have held, and perhaps still hold, about what a Catholic is and what he believes. I quickly and openly add that many of these misconceptions are not due to Protestant prejudice but are rooted in the fact that Protestants have seen, heard, or read a number of Catholics whose understanding of their own faith was not central enough or sure enough. Many Protestant misconceptions of Roman Catholicism are directly due to Catholic misconceptions of their own faith.

One major misconception of Roman Catholic belief, held by many Protestants because it was lived by many Catholics, is that

Roman Catholics worship the Blessed Virgin Mary. Official Roman Catholic teaching has never presented Mary as divine; as a consequence Roman Catholic teaching has not only never encouraged the worship of Mary but has strictly forbidden it. Nevertheless, this is not always obvious. Consider, for example, the experience of a Protestant visiting a Catholic country in the Spanish tradition, or seeing a procession honoring Mary in an Italian-American neighborhood. Such an observer might well conclude that the flowers surrounding the statue of Mary, the hymns, the atmosphere combining both celebration and religious devotion, could be explained only if the participants were honoring a divine being. We shall see in chapter 10 what the Roman Catholic theology of the Blessed Virgin Mary actually is. For the present, we wish simply to clear up the widespread misconception that Catholics worship Mary or consider her divine.

Mary has meaning for the Christian only in her relationship to the Holy Trinity. She was and is a creature, like ourselves except in her perfect fidelity to the will of God. This, however, is not to deny certain facts. In the early Middle Ages and in certain countries even in our own time, notably countries of Hispanic cultural influence, there have developed alongside the proper honor and devotion given to Mary an emotionalism and flamboyance which could be easily confused with worship. Often, for Hispanic Catholics, there has been an excess of devotion amounting almost to superstition.

Another widespread Protestant misconception should also be dealt with here, just after we have entered the house of Catholic belief. It is that misconception which claims, or at least suggests, that Roman Catholics think the Pope to be incapable of sin. Roman Catholics do believe in Papal infallibility—that the Pope, as the successor to Christ, cannot teach falsely when, in a most sacred and solemn manner, he enunciates a truth to the entire Church concerning Christian faith and morality. Papal infallibility is light years away from Papal *impeccability*—which would mean that the Pope was incapable of committing sin.

In chapter 6 we shall attempt to set forth what Catholics believe on the score of Papal infallibility. All that we wish to do at this point is to set aside the misconception of Papal impeccability. Catholic historians, as well as Protestant, have not hesitated to chronicle the lives of many Popes who were far from sinless. There is no need here to go into a list of such unworthy Popes, nor to chronicle their lapses from grace. Suffice it to say that even one such Pope would be too many, and there have been more than one. The fact, however, that some Popes have been far less than perfect does not in the least diminish their spiritual authority. We have only to recall the position of preeminence given to St. Peter by Christ Himself, to realize that spiritual authority within the Christian Church does not always nor necessarily depend upon the sinlessness or even high virtue of the one to whom such privileged place is given.

Perhaps no other aspect of Roman Catholic life has so baffled Protestants, or led to so many misconceptions, as has the Catholic practice of oral confession. Almost every Protestant has heard of, and many have actually seen, the confessional boxes in Catholic Churches. The priest sits in the middle of what looks like a voting booth, with curtains covering the entrance on either side. The person "going to confession" or making his confession enters through the curtains, kneels down, and confesses the sins of which he feels himself guilty. We shall, in chapter 10, discuss the Catholic theology of confession and the Sacrament of Penance. At this point, we wish to state, merely, not what confession is but what it is not. Confession is not an exercise in Christian mumbo jumbo, nor does it represent, in the Catholic view, the interposition of another human being between a sinful creature and the Creator whom his sins have offended. No Catholic who truly understands the nature and meaning of confession would ever feel that he could do what he wanted so long as he went to confession.

Confession is not that easy for the Catholic. It represents, or should, serious soul-searching before one enters the confessional. Unless the penitent has resolved not to sin again or is not truly sorry for his sins, then he knows that his sins will not be forgiven. He may fool the priest sitting in the darkened confessional into whose ear he pours out the story of his faults, failings, and sins, but he cannot fool Christ to whom he is actually confessing through the person of the priest.

Nor does the Catholic pay to go to confession. He pays, of course, the coin of humility and remorse, but he does not pay money. The forgiveness of sin through the use of the Sacrament of Penance is one of those spiritual services to which the Roman Catholic has the right, in terms of Church law. For a priest either to expect or to demand payment would be in itself a sinful action on the part of the priest.

The last two misconceptions with which we shall deal touch more personally the life of the Protestant. The first misconception asserts that Roman Catholics feel that any one not blessed by being a member of the Roman Catholic Church cannot hope to attain salvation. Exactly the opposite is true. The Church has always taught that the conscience of the individual is the guide which the individual must follow. If a person were to become sincerely convinced that the Roman Catholic Church were not of divine origin and that another Church were, he would be obliged in conscience to forsake Catholicism and to embrace that Church which he thought truly to represent Christ's will for men.

This teaching on the primacy of the individual conscience has been upheld in other but equally forceful ways by the Church itself. A particular example in fairly recent American history may serve to illustrate the point. In 1950, a well-known American Jesuit priest, Rev. Francis Feeney, began to teach and preach that anyone outside the visible Catholic Church could not be saved. Father Feeney was an eloquent speaker and had, in the years previous, achieved an enviable reputation in the American Catholic community for his winning wit as well as for his ability to express Catholic teachings in a forceful and persuasive manner. When he began, therefore, to teach that there was no salvation outside the Catholic Church, his words had an influence considerably greater than would have had the words of a less gifted, less well-known priest. Father Feeney had attracted large crowds to the outdoor sermons which he regularly preached on Sunday afternoons on the Boston Commons. When he began to fulminate against those outside the Catholic Church and to close the gates of salvation to them with a loud clang, he was ordered by Archbishop (now Cardinal) Cushing of Boston to stop his erroneous preaching. When Father Feeney refused to do so, the case was taken to Rome. The Holy Office protested against Father Feeney's interpretation of this point of Catholic teaching, but Father Feeney still refused to recant, or at least to be silent. He was excommunicated by Rome from the Catholic Church—thereby finding himself, ironically, in terms of his own teaching outside the possibility of salvation.

Up to this point, we have been discussing widespread Protestant myths and misconceptions about the teachings and practices of the Roman Catholic Church. Thus, we have distinguished between Papal infallibility and impeccability. We have seen that Catholics who knew their faith never worshiped Mary and that the Catholic Church has always recognized, at least in theory, the primary importance of the individual's conscience over the teaching authority of the Church. All of this aims simply to show the Protestant reader why he will not find exhibited in the Catholic "House of Faith" certain rather frightening features that he might well have expected to see.

There are, however, within Roman Catholicism certain exhibits which we Catholics at the moment are rather hurriedly removing from view—in much the same way that a museum director removes from view paintings "by" Renoir or Rembrandt which he has discovered to be spurious.

On the walls of Roman Catholicism there have hung, until quite recently, a number of paintings which were purchased and hung in the sincere conviction that they represented authentic depictions of the basic Christian faith. Lately, however, historians and scholars from both Protestantism and Catholicism have indi-

cated that these "paintings" were not authentic and therefore did
not represent a work done by the Master or any of His immediate
school.

Before these paintings are removed, however, it is only fair
that we Roman Catholics look carefully at them ourselves and
try to give a reasonable explanation of why they once were hung,
in places of honor, upon our walls. It is to this exhibit then, of
outdated—but once real—questions that we shall turn in the next
chapter.

3

Outdated Questions

In approaching the subject of this chapter, one is reminded of an incident which took place several years ago. The then-director of the budget for the Department of Defense was undergoing a very demanding questioning by a Senate Committee. When a member of the Senate Committee asked a particularly difficult question, the budget director took off into the wide blue sky. In his response, he flew above the question, around the question, and below the question. After several minutes of exhibiting his ability to evade, like a high flying hawk, the pellets of his questioner, the budget director stopped. He reflected a moment, and then turned to his top aide and said, "George, am I trying to evade a question for which we *do* have an answer?"

Roman Catholics have often found themselves, in the last several years, in much the same position as that of the budget director. We may offer involved answers to questions without realizing that the questions themselves permit very simple answers. It is this type of question—once, perhaps, a very real one but now outmoded—which we shall consider in this chapter.

For many centuries, those Protestants who bothered even to concern themselves about it were most understandably indignant at the realization that the Roman Catholic Church officially called them "heretics." The name of heretic is one which no serious Christian could accept calmly and philosophically, for the word itself means, in the Greek, "one who picks and chooses." The word has, at certain times within the history of Christianity, been accurately applied to those who did "pick and choose" among the teachings of the Christian Church. Thus Marcion in the third century chose, without any support from Christian tradition, to regard the Jewish Scriptures, the Old Testament, to be meaningless for the Christian. In Marcion's view, the Old Testament had been, not fulfilled, but completely abrogated by the New—in somewhat the same way that the Constitution of the United States abrogated all of the laws of the British Parliament which had once been applicable to the Colonial States in America. Marcion was, then, a heretic precisely because he picked and chose among Christian teachings those which best fit his own ideas of reality.

Similarly, Arius and his followers in the fourth century were heretics. They picked among the various possible explanations of the nature of Jesus Christ and chose the explanation directly opposed to the common faith of the Christian community. Arius taught that Jesus Christ was not divine, not the Son of God, the Word Incarnate, but was rather the most sublime of creatures, occupying, as it were, a middle place between God and man. As a creature, he was infinitely below God; as the finest representative of the human race, he was measurably above most men.

Those men who founded the major branches of Protestant belief were convinced that, far from picking and choosing among the truths of Christianity, they were attempting to assert the fulness of Christian revelation. The Roman Catholic Church once called these men heretics—Luther, Calvin, Zwingli, Hus and many others. This simply indicates how blinded the Church had become to an authentic understanding of what God had revealed in Christ Jesus and, through Him, had entrusted to the men of every subsequent generation. For centuries, in fact, the Roman Catholic Church after the Reformation did, indeed, call those who did not profess allegiance to Rome "heretics"—pickers and choosers of Christian truths. In the Roman Catholic liturgy of Good Friday, for example, there was, until quite recently, a prayer for heretics. It was obvious to Roman Catholics hearing this prayer that they were, indeed, praying for their Protestant friends, neighbors, or perhaps mother-in-law or wife.

Now, however, the well-informed Catholic, when asked why he considers Protestants to be heretics, can give the direct, simple answer that he does not so consider them. Instead of gunning his engine and heading for the blue sky, he can remain on solid ground. Pope John XXIII, shortly after he assumed office, ordered stricken from the Roman Catholic liturgy every phrase which could possibly give offense to those not of the Roman Catholic Communion. He thus ordered removed from Catholic liturgy references to the Jews which suggested that they had been culpably responsible for their rejection of Jesus, not only during His lifetime in Palestine, but through all of the centuries since.

Pope John also struck from the Catholic liturgy any reference to other Christians as "heretics." They were, Pope John insisted, separated brothers of the Roman Catholic—and he hastened to point out that the bricks forming the walls of separation had been fashioned and mortared into place by the Catholics as well as by the Protestants. The Second Vatican Council followed the spirit of Pope John's attitude of recognizing both the sincerity of the non-Catholic and the shortcomings of the Catholics. In its decrees on Ecumenism and on the Church the Council did not once refer to Protestants as heretics. Indeed, on a more positive note, it recognized, for the first time since the Reformation, that Protestant churches were, in fact, authentic Christian churches and shared in the richness of the life of the Triune God imparted to man.

As a Roman Catholic, I could wish that all of the offenses against Christian charity exhibited in the antagonism and hostility of one church to another had been, for the greatest part, the fault of the Roman Catholic Church. When we Christians pray, "forgive us our trespasses," we genuinely hope that we will have little to report in the next phrase, "as we forgive those who trespass against us." While we recognize our own sins and sinfulness, we would prefer to bear the burden of guilt and would hope that there would be few, if any, who had been guilty toward us.

It is a matter of historical fact, however, that the Christian churches have been separated from one another, not only by their differing understanding of this or that aspect of the Christian revelation; they have also—and more grievously—been separated by mutual suspicion and active enmity. Our American history shows how, almost from the very beginning, Christians who came to these shores seeking religious freedom carved both a culture and a Church out of the wilderness. They did, indeed, find here religious freedom, but many of them promptly denied this freedom to others. The early treatment of Baptists in the Massachusetts Bay Colony is but one of many instances wherein those who came to America to worship God in their own way came quickly also to assert that their way was the only way. Just as the Baptists were driven from Massachusetts, members of many churches found themselves unwelcome in other colonies where there was, either tacitly or explicitly, a "state" religion.

Just as the Roman Catholic Church, then, has in the tragic past viewed other Christian churches with animosity, so too, many of the Protestant churches have viewed both Roman Catholicism and other Protestant denominations with the same animosity.

This failure of Christian love, so often fostered by the churches themselves, has been epitomized for me in the experience of a very close friend now in her seventies. She was born in a medium-sized city in the Midwest, and was baptized an Episcopalian. She was a very devout person and from her early teens devoted much of her time to church work: teaching Sunday School to poor children, playing the organ at religious services, tending the altar and its appointments in preparation for worship.

On a visit to the East in her late teens, she attended Episcopal services with her cousin and was surprised to see how the service in a High Episcopalian Church was closer to that of Catholic services than to the Low Church Episcopal liturgy back home. When, upon her return, she commented upon this difference to her Episcopal pastor, he dismissed the High Episcopal wing of his church with a sniff, indicating that High Episcopalians were really no better than Roman Catholics. In the meantime, because of her religious interest and concern, the young lady began to read widely in church history. As a result of her reading, she concluded that, for her, the Roman Catholic Church represented Christianity more authentically than did her own communion. As a consequence, to the distress of her family, friends—and pastor—she was received into the Catholic Church.

Some months later she met and married a Roman Catholic stationed in her native city for military duty. The year was 1918, and her experience was not unlike that of many others in that period, or indeed, in the decades since. When she went with her fiance to meet his family, his mother drew her aside and asked her not to mention to other members of the family that she was a "convert" to Catholicism, and assured the young lady that she would keep this fact secret. My friend pointed out that she was proud to have been an Episcopalian, and viewed Roman Catholicism as but a logical development in her effort to live a Christian life. The older woman was, of course, taken aback and neither she nor her family could, in their relations over many years, fully forget the fact that one of their own had married a "convert," rather than a "cradle" Catholic.

Here, then, we have a situation which typifies the strained relations between the different Christian churches, relations which have caused individuals unnecessary anguish. Such relations have also served to establish a credibility gap between the Christian churches and non-Christians, who have so often looked in vain for signs of that Christian love which is supposed to be the beating heart of Christian witness.

One can easily imagine the pain of a young girl who is looked upon by her family, friends, and pastor as though she had committed a crime by following her conscience and joining the Catholic Church. The pain would be no less when her Catholic mother-in-law and her new family would treat her as though she were somehow but a second-class Catholic because she had read and thought her way into the Church rather than having had the good sense to be born into it.

The story has, however, something of a happy ending. My friend recently attended the wedding of her grandniece, a Protestant who was marrying a Roman Catholic. No hostility was shown by either family at the fact that the bride and groom were each marrying "outside their Church." The wedding ceremony was conducted in a Roman Catholic Church, but the bride's Episcopal pastor officiated at the exchange of vows side by side with the Catholic priest. It was no surprise for my friend to learn afterwards that the pastor and the priest were good friends who had worked together on many projects in the city involving Protestants, Catholics—and Jews.

It is very interesting to reflect that the very things which God had used to join men together have been used by men to rend them asunder from other men. We believe that there is a merciful, loving God Who sent His only begotten Son to earth as proof of his love for man. This belief should have served to make all Christians one in heart, even when they have chosen, for whatever reason, to display their common belief in diverse forms of cult, worship, and service. Unfortunately, we Christians must all face up to the fact that we have accepted the Scriptures as God speaking to man, yet because of our perversity and pride have made the Bible sound like voices coming from the Tower of Babel.

Let me give but one example. During the Second Vatican Council, which ran from December, 1961, to December, 1965, each session was preceeded by a Mass in St. Peter's Basilica. After the Mass, the formal session of the Council would begin. Up the long aisle of St. Peter's would come a group of bishops carrying in sacred and solemn procession a copy of the Bible. These were flanked by other bishops carrying lighted candles to indicate that the Bible was, in itself, God present among men even as He had been present among men, in Catholic belief, through the celebration of the Eucharist completed moments before. The procession, of which the Bible was the center, would move to the high altar of St. Peter's and there, upon the altar designed by Bernini, the Bible was enthroned.

The significance of this ceremony was that whatever the bishops who formed the Council were to think or say was to be done under the magisterial rule of God's Word—that Word which enlightens the human mind, corrects the human mind, and directs it.

In other words, this ceremony, which had been a part of every previous Council of the Roman Catholic Church, was to indicate the Church's recognition that it had been born from the womb of the Scriptures. The Council's essential task was not only to proclaim the Word of God to all men, but to constantly scrutinize its own deliberations, thoughts, and actions to make sure that the Church itself was faithful to the Word of God. The Bible, enthroned amid all the solemn pageantry and serious discussions of the Council, reminded those bishops present that God was in their midst: God the Father, Creator and fashioner of mankind; Jesus Christ, the Incarnate Word, upon whom the Church was founded; the Holy Spirit, promised by Christ to the Church as the source of sanctity and enlightenment.

Many Protestant theologians and church officials had been invited to attend the Second Vatican Council as observers to its proceedings. Apart from not being able to vote, these Protestant observers could take part in every session of the Council. They were given the drafts of documents under discussion and had the opportunity to present their own points of view to Catholic theologians and bishops whose deliberations were serving to shape the Church for the next several generations. I have had the privilege of knowing a number of these Protestant observers. Each has expressed not only to me but in articles and books, his gratified surprise that the once-closed Catholic Church would invite non-Catholics to observe so closely and take part in the Church's highest official deliberations.

All of this is much as though the U.S. Secretary of State should be invited to observe a meeting of the Soviet Central Committee. Yet each of these Protestant observers pointed out that even more surprising than their having been invited to the highest sessions of the Church was the daily enthronement of the Scriptures upon the altar of St. Peter's. They had not realized, these Protestant observers said, that the Roman Catholic Church put the Word of God above the Word of the Church itself, or regarded the Scriptures as embodying the imperatives of the Triune God for the Church founded upon Christ.

I can readily understand the fact that even knowledgeable Protestant theologians and church officials would be surprised to learn that the Catholic Church held the Scriptures in as sacred regard as did the Protestants themselves. It must also be pointed out, however, that many Roman Catholics, if they had had the happy privilege of the Protestant observers to witness the enthronement of the Bible on the altar of St. Peter's would, in all probability, have missed the rich symbolic meaning. Many would have been equally surprised to learn that within Roman Catholicism the Scriptures are, indeed, a source, center, and rule of faith.

The reason why so many Catholics are, even today, ignorant of the Scriptures and their role within Catholic belief is simply because the Church, through several centuries after the Reformation, adopted a very cautious attitude toward scriptural reading by the Roman Catholic who was not equipped to interpret the Scriptures as he read. However from the time of Pope Leo XIII (1870–1903), Roman Catholics had been encouraged to read the Scriptures privately. Special blessings were offered to the Roman Catholics who would spend fifteen minutes a day reading the Bible—any portion of any book, even without a priest peering over his shoulder to make sure that the Catholic did not misinterpret what he was reading. The fact is, however, that in the area of Bible reading, as in the area of social thought and action, the Popes were far ahead, not only of the lay people, but of most priests and bishops. For the average Catholic, there remained the belief that he should avoid Bible reading, a heritage of the Protestant-Catholic polemics of the centuries after the Reformation. Not only could the "devil cite Scripture for his purpose," but insisting on any "right" of "private interpretation" was rejected as Protestant. The whole development of Scripture reading, under the guidance of the Holy Spirit, which has so enriched Protestantism was thus largely lost within the Roman Catholic Church. Even Protestants themselves, of course, recognized that the Holy Spirit, in the case of certain aberrant sects like the Diggers, seemed to have come up with strange interpretations indeed.

Here, again, both Protestant and Catholic must recognize their historical failures in love one toward the other. In argument and discussion, the Catholic would delight in bringing up the Diggers, the Shakers, and other obviously fanatic sects within Protestantism. By this, it was suggested that the misguided fringe really represented the typical example of what happens if the Scriptures are read and interpreted by the individual. Interpretations that such individuals believe to be the guidance of the Holy Spirit can be seen as reading in the Scriptures what the interpreter wishes to read.

On the other hand, Protestants, in this unlovely and unloving kind of debate, would make much of the fact that copies of the Scriptures were chained to pillars in medieval cathedrals. This type of argument suggests that Catholics, even before the Reformation, were discouraged from reading the Bible. It conveniently overlooks the fact that, in the ages before printing, handwritten manuscripts of the Bible could take thousands of man-hours and the skins of a large flock of sheep. As a consequence, one manuscript of the entire Bible would have a monetary value, in our terms, of thousands of dollars. Its purchase would be a considerable outlay for the people of a town. They were not prepared to accept calmly the possibility of a believer's (or more likely, an unbeliever's) walking off with their only copy of the Bible, a copy which would have as high a market value elsewhere as a small Rembrandt stolen today from a museum.

It is not true, then, in the absolute sense that the Catholic Church has either forbidden or discouraged the reading of the Scriptures. Indeed, as we have indicated above, Catholics have been encouraged to read the Scriptures daily. Moreover, in every Mass there took place an enthronement of the Bible similar to that which took place in St. Peter's Basilica before the opening of each session of the Council. In the past, the real meaning of this enthronement of the Scriptures in the celebration of Mass was really lost upon most priests and their people. Until the last twenty years, then, the Scriptures held, within Roman Catholic thought and practice, a strange and rather paradoxical position.

The best way in which I, at least, can explain this paradoxical position is to recall a recent experience. I had been invited to Texas to take part in a conference, involving Catholics and Protestants, on the place of the Eucharist in our respective Churches. While waiting in the Austin airport for the people who were to drive me into the ranch-country where the conference took place, I noticed in an Austin paper the following news story:

The local television station in a small town in western Texas experienced technical problems in transmitting the picture. In place of the usual neatly printed slide informing the viewer of this fact, there appeared on the screen a hand holding up a hand-written sign which read: "Due to technical difficulties we are temporarily unable to bring you the picture. We have also temporarily lost the slide used to inform you of this fact. Please bear with us."

We Roman Catholics, for more than a century, have "lost the picture" as far as the role of the Scriptures in the Christian life are concerned. This has not been due to the teaching and exhortation of the Church on its highest levels, beginning with the Pope. The failure of the average Catholic to grasp and practice what the Church was telling him is simply another indication of the gap which exists, perhaps in every Church but certainly within Roman Catholicism, between the best official expressions of what the Church means and what its adherents prefer it to mean. The Communist regimes everywhere do a far better job of getting their people to follow "the party line" than the Church has ever been able to manage. From the late nineteenth century to the present day, the Roman Catholic Church has been attempting to waken the conscience of the Roman Catholic to his responsibility for world justice, peace, and aid to the poor, the disenfranchised, the discriminated against everywhere. Through all these years, some bishops, many priests, and thousands of lay people have either tried to explain that the Church did not really mean what it seemed to mean in these "hard sayings," or was misinformed about the realities of injustice, degradation, and deprivation which the Church was attempting to heal. A classic expression of this attitude occurred when Pope John XXIII in an encyclical entitled *Mater et Magistra,* issued a stirring call for Catholics to involve themselves in the struggle for world peace and justice. A very prominent Roman Catholic journalist, William F. Buckley, Jr., wrote a lead editorial in *The National Review* headed, "Mater Si; Magister Non."

William Buckley's editorial presented a scathing attack upon Pope John's declaration that Christians should be in the forefront of the efforts to solve the world's ills. It is his conviction that the Church should talk to man about "spiritual things," but that it had no right to enter into the realm of "politics"—either national or international. It is obvious, I think, that Jesus Christ, God and Man, through His life, death, and resurrection, dissolved not only the distinction between Jew and Gentile, barbarian and Greek, slave and free, but that He also dissolved the distinction between politics and spiritual things, between this world and the next, between the sanctuary and the street. To the Christian, listening with his heart to Christ's own words, Christ is to be found particularly in the person of those who suffer—the poor, the hungry, the thirsty, those in prison. He has promised astonishing rewards for a cup of cold water given in His name. Certainly, the Church has not only the right, but the obligation, to make clear what a cup of cold water means in the concrete circumstances of our day. The poor in Appalachia and in our urban ghettoes need the cold water of full economic opportunity. Those peoples in Africa and Asia who are struggling to free themselves from the invisible chains of colonialism need the cold water of economic and technological assistance which can be offered to them by the advanced, have-nations of the North Atlantic, historically Christian, white community. For Pope John to have pointed out the particular demands of these situations upon the Christian conscience should not have invoked the kind of brittle, pseudosophisticated response of "Mother, yes—Teacher, no."

On the other hand, the willingness of Roman Catholics to follow, almost blindly, some practices and teachings of Roman Catholicism which were of secondary importance while yet reserving the right to reject the Church's evangelical exhortation to feed the hungry and clothe the naked obviously indicate the type of distorted values which has marked Roman Catholicism. It was not a Protestant, not a cynical Catholic, but an extremely intelligent and concerned Roman Catholic bishop who remarked, after the atomic bombs had been dropped on Nagasaki and Hiroshima: "Thousands of people have been slain in a single night, with very few protests from Roman Catholics except the protest registered by the Pope and a few theologians. Can you imagine the outcries from Catholics, however, if instead of atomic bombs, the United States had dropped millions of contraceptives upon Japan?"

Roman Catholics, then, have a very difficult time in keeping two thoughts together in their minds. When they succeed in keeping two ideas together in the confines of their minds, they are quite likely to put the more important idea second and the less important one first. It is clear to anyone who has studied the problem at all that the challenge to feed the hungry, give drink to the thirsty, etc., has been laid upon the conscience of his followers by Jesus Christ Himself. On the other hand, the Church's traditional opposition to artificial contraception is based not upon the Scriptures but upon the writings of theologians, beginning with St. Augustine in the fourth century.

As a result of many factors, Catholics can now begin to be able to keep two ideas together at the same time and, somewhat painfully, to put the first idea before the second. Because this process is taking place, we have been able to deal in this chapter with what we have called "Outdated Questions"—points of view the Church once held but which it has either changed or is in the process of changing. For this reason, so far as the house of the Roman Catholic Faith is concerned, we have been standing in a replica of a Victorian parlor. The room is elegantly furnished, with heavy drapes which never permit the sun to enter. The over-stuffed horsehair furniture is protected, by antimacassars, from the soil of human occupancy; in the corner stands the harmonium, always carefully dusted but played only on special occasions like weddings and funerals.

It is a pleasure for the Catholic to leave the well-appointed but unused parlor and move into another room—in fact, the most important room of the house.

4

The Dining Room

As we enter this room, I am afraid that I must apologize for the fact that it is in the process of renovation. The dining table, which had once been very ornate, where possible made of marble, and affixed to the wall, is now being dismantled and replaced by a simple wooden table placed in the center of the room.

The organ still remains in place, but one can also notice that there are some guitars resting against it.

It may seem somewhat surprising—if not shocking—to speak of the place where Catholics worship as a dining room. But I know of no better way to illustrate the profound changes which have taken place over the last ten years in what we Catholics call the liturgy. The word "liturgy" is not used as much by Protestants as by Catholics and may call for a brief explanation. The word itself comes from two Greek words, and means literally, "the work of the people."

This expression is a very revealing one, so far as the understanding of Catholic worship is concerned. The principal public act of worship in the Church is the celebration of the Eucharist, more familarly called the Mass. The Mass is the "work of the people"—it is the prayer offered to God by the community of Christians assembled to worship Him. The offering of the Mass depends on the presence of a priest. In the Roman Catholic view, Christ, the Great High Priest, in the Mass offers Himself to the Father. He is the unique Priest (bridge-builder) between God and man, since He alone is both human and divine. All baptized Catholics, however, share in this one priesthood which is Christ's. The ordained priest participates in the priesthood of Christ in a special way because he has been summoned by Christ, and ordained by the Church, to perform the tasks of a priest within, and for, the Roman Catholic community. All of the laity, however, have been called, through Baptism, to the priesthood of the faithful. They, too, have the responsibility of serving as priests—performing the tasks of bridge-building and offering sacrifice—toward each other member of the Catholic community and to the world.

When the liturgy is celebrated, then, it represents an assembly of priests: Christ the High Priest, Whose own Body and Blood is re-presented to the Father in oblation through the human agency of a consecrated human priest or priests and the lay men and women who are members of Christ's Body, which is the Church.

But the Mass is not only a sacrificial oblation; it is also a banquet, a family meal. Roman Catholics believe (as do many Protestants) that Jesus Christ, God and Man, is truly present in the bread and wine after a consecrated minister has spoken over the bread and wine the words of Consecration: "This is My Body; This is My Blood." Through his reception of the Body and the Blood, the Catholic believes that he is nourished spiritually by that upon which he has fed. As a consequence, he has deepened his union with Christ by sharing in the Divine Life called Grace. The Mass, then, is seen as "doing what Christ did" at the Last Supper, and doing it precisely because Christ commanded that it be done, and empowered His Apostles and their successors through all time to transform bread and wine into His Own Flesh and Blood.

Obviously, Christians have disagreed, and continue to disagree, on the interpretation of the texts in the New Testament concerning Christ's institution of the Lord's Supper. It is not our intention here to replay these arguments but simply to state the Roman Catholic belief in the Eucharist, the Lord's Supper, and attempt to explain what this belief means in the life of the Catholic. It is also true that Roman Catholics themselves have not always kept clearly in mind each of the components in their complex theology of the Eucharist. Thus, for example, there was a tendency to maximize the understanding of the Mass as Sacrifice and to minimize that aspect of the Eucharist which saw it as a Sacred Meal, the Christian's Passover Banquet. There was also, until the very recent past, a reluctance within Roman Catholicism to give the priesthood of the faithful its proper place.

In both cases, neglecting the Mass as Sacred Meal and de-emphasizing the priesthood of the faithful represented a Catholic reaction to much of Protestant thought on these points. Since Protestants emphasized the Lord's Supper as memorial banquet, and underlined the priesthood of all believers, Catholics became anxious not to adopt Protestant points of view—and as a result all but lost a great deal of a central Christian understanding of the rich heritage embodied in the Eucharist and, indeed, the understanding of the Church.

We shall return, in a later chapter, to the role of the lay person in the Catholic Church, the importance of which has been strongly reemphasized by the Second Vatican Council. Our principal concern here, however, is with the Church's understanding of the Mass.

It must be pointed out that, no matter how the Church, in a given period, failed to keep firmly fixed in mind the *total* picture, it has always maintained a firm faith in the Real Presence of Christ in the Eucharist. It has always regarded the Mass as the supreme act of worship which can be paid to God precisely because it has always insisted that in this act of worship Christ is the Supreme Priest. It is only in virtue of His priestliness that the consecrated human minister has the power effectively to repeat Christ's own words, making of bread His Body, of wine His Blood.

Because of this conviction, there grew up a statement centuries ago by which Catholics affirmed, "it is the Mass that matters." Far more than most statements by the Popes on various matters, far more than whether or not there were Catholic schools, far more than whether the Church enjoyed privilege or suffered persecution within a given country, it was, indeed, the Mass that mattered. In the Mass, Catholics, caught up in Christ, were able to re-present the Sacrifice of Calvary to the Father. They received within their very being the same Christ Who had died on Calvary, rose from the rock tomb, and had returned to the Father to make constant intercession for us.

Under Elizabeth I, the sacrifice of the Mass was forbidden in England. Any priest caught celebrating Mass was usually killed as a traitor; Catholics caught attending Mass were fined and or imprisoned. Yet through those tragic years, the Mass continued to be celebrated throughout England, in secrecy, of course, and in very unlikely places. Many Priests gave their lives for having said Mass, and many Catholics were impoverished because they had attended Mass. But for the Catholic, reading of these bloodstained pages of history serves but to deepen his own realization that it *is* the Mass that matters, that the Eucharist is the very heart and center of his Christian living.

A well-known Protestant theologian once told me, at an ecumenical conference, that he had learned more about Catholicism by attending several Masses than he had learned from reading Catholic theological manuals. I believe that most Catholics would also say that they have really learned more about the nature of their belief from the celebration of the liturgy than from their formal study of Catholic theology. All of this, I realize, will be simply baffling or irritating to a Protestant who has not attended a Catholic Mass but is anxious to know something of what the Mass means to a Catholic. The Mass, however, is basically an experience, an encounter with God and an encounter with those who share our Catholic community of faith—and as we all know, it is impossible to communicate the fulness of an experience to others. How can a mother express in words what she feels when she holds her first child in her arms? How can this same child, grown to adulthood, convey in words to his mother all that he feels about the girl he has met and hopes to marry? It is with something close to despair, then, that I attempt to set forth in words what the Mass is to a Catholic. I realize, even more deeply than will the Protestant reader, how cold and merely ritualistic the Mass seems when it is described rather than experienced. But we must at least make the attempt. . . .

The celebration of the Eucharist begins with the *Entrance Rite*. As the priest or priests who are to preside at the Mass leave the sanctuary to come to the altar, the congregation sings a hymn. Until the liturgical changes of several years ago, this procession to the altar was accompanied by a hymn sung by the choir or, if there were no choir, it was accompanied by heavy silence from the congregation, and was executed with great foot speed by the priest. Now, however, we Catholics have learned to sing.

It would be unquestionably more accurate to say, not that we Catholics have learned to sing, but that we now have more congregational hymning than we used to have. Many of these hymns have, indeed, been borrowed from Protestants, and I personally feel that a number of them have been taken from the Protestants' liturgical litter basket. The intention behind the congregational singing is, however, clear enough and valid enough: to encourage the active participation of the congregation in Divine Worship, rather than to have them mere spectators at the sacred drama of the Mass.

When the priest has come to the altar, he uses prayers drawn from the Psalms which are intended to prepare both the priest and the people for the solemn event which they are to share together. Part of this preparation consists in the priest's confessing his sinfulness to the congregation, and the congregation's expressing its sinfulness and weakness (using the same prayer) to the priest. Unfortunately, in most cases the congregation is still singing the Entrance Hymn at this point, and the note of dialogue between priest and congregation is drowned out by the valiant but often ragged efforts of the congregation to complete the Entrance Hymn.

The priest then ascends to the altar table and kisses it. In the

Catholic tradition the altar table is reverenced, not only because
it is the altar of sacrifice and the table which holds the Sacred
Banquet, but because it is also a symbol of Christ Himself. The
priest then descends from the altar to the left side of the sanctuary. He then leads the congregation in their joint prayer of
praise to the Triune God—an ancient prayer, the *Gloria,* which
reechoes the greeting of the angels to the shepherds announcing
the birth of Christ:

Glory to God in the highest.
And on earth peace to the men he loves.
We praise you.
We bless you.
We adore you.
We glorify you.
We give you thanks for your great glory.
O Lord God, heavenly King, God the Father Almighty.
O Lord Jesus Christ, the only-begotten Son.
Lord God, Lamb of God, Son of the Father.
You who take away the sins
of the world, have mercy on us.
You who take away the sins
of the world, receive our prayer.
You who sit at the right hand of
the Father, have mercy on us.
For you alone are holy.
You alone are the Lord.
You alone, O Jesus Christ, are most high.
Together with the Holy Spirit
in the glory of God the Father.   Amen

The priest then recites the assigned prayer for the day, a prayer
which represents the plea of the entire assembly, asking God's
special blessing in relation to the recurring needs of mankind for
greater strength, greater generosity, or greater vision.

At this point there begins the *Celebration of the Word.* This
part of the Mass consists of readings from the Sacred Scriptures.

The first part of these readings is drawn from either the Old
Testament or from the Epistles or Acts of the Apostles in the
New Testament. The priest read these selections, in Latin, until
the changes in the liturgy were instituted several years ago. Now
it is customary for a layman to give these readings, while both the
celebrating priest and the congregation listen as the selections are
read—in English. An important change has obviously taken place
here. The fact that a layman now proclaims this portion of the
Word of God signifies the fact that the laity, too, share in the
liturgy. The fact that the priest listens to the reading, along with
the congregation, signifies that he, too, is a member of the people
of God. He is not only a herald of the Word, but must also be a
hearer and doer of the Word, even as must be the remainder of
the assembly over which he presides in the office of special love
and special service.

We might pause here, briefly, to reflect on what we have just
seen and heard. It is already obvious that the Church, through its
incorporation into the Mass of psalms and Scripture readings, does
indeed not only reverence the Word of God, but also makes it a
rule of faith and action. While the individual Catholic, as we have
seen, is encouraged to read the Scriptures as an individual, he is
also summoned to hear the Word of God proclaimed in the assembly of worship. The Church has always enshrined the Scriptures in her liturgy—literally, through having a copy of the
Scriptures placed on the altar but also by proclaiming the Word
as one of the central parts of her worship service.

We might note also that this first part of the Mass, the *Celebration of the Word,* is in itself drawn from the synagogue service of
Israel and shows the continuity between the people of the First
Covenant and the people of the Second. The Jews still assemble
to hear and meditate on God's message, as He had taught them to
do. Jesus Himself, it will be recalled, took part in precisely such
a service, and He chose the reading of Isaiah in the synagogue on
the sabbath as the occasion when He first announced His own
mission (Luke 4: 16–22).

Our Lord, in the Jewish understanding, would have been a

"layman" in the synagogue. Although neither priest nor scribe, He had been invited to read the Scripture passage assigned for that particular sabbath. Roman Catholic laymen now read the first portion of the Scriptures to the assembly—a task and a privilege which had been denied them until the liturgical revisions of several years ago.

After the first Scripture reading, the priest, who has been listening to the proclamation of the Word, now comes forward himself to proclaim the good news of the Gospel through his reading of an appointed section. After this reading, the priest then preaches a homily, a short sermon based on the portion of the Gospel just read or the Scripture passage contained in the first reading. The sermon has never assumed the importance in Roman Catholic liturgy that it holds in most Protestant services of worship. There has developed, however, a widespread realization that preaching is, indeed, part of the essential task of the priest, for which he can expect special divine assistance. As a result, sermons in Catholic Churches have improved, are more rooted in Scripture than in the personal preoccupations of the preacher, and yet remain mercifully brief.

Through the Celebration of the Word, the Catholic believes that God has spoken to him. For many Protestants, God speaks (or is at least willing to speak) whenever one reads the Word of God. The Catholic, too, has recently and slowly come to accept this same reality of the living Word of the living God, forever ready to break into the history of the individual Christian. In the Mass, however, the Roman Catholic hears the Word of God not only as an individual, but as the member of a community. Together, we are all comforted, we are all enlightened, we are all challenged. The proclamation, made by both a layman and a priest, of God's Word makes God present in our midst. As He has ever done in His relations with man, God has taken the initiative, God has come to meet man, God has spoken to man. In this portion of the Mass, we all—priest and people—have listened to the message and the summons of God present among us through His Word.

In the portion of the Mass which follows, the community responds to God's message and answers His summons. With God present in our midst through His Word, we attempt to make ourselves present to Him through our words in that portion of the Mass which is called the *Celebration of the Eucharist.*

The first prayer (our words responding to God's Word) is the Profession of Faith. In the Mass, we repeat the words of the centuries-old Nicene Creed, with which Christians since the fourth century have affirmed their belief in the Trinity and, as a consequence, their full belief in the complete divinity and humanity of Jesus Christ. Many Protestant communities, who fear that creeds and confessions are wax upon the wings of the Holy Spirit, do not employ such a statement of faith in their public services of worship. It is interesting to note, however, that the Nicene Creed, recited by Roman Catholics in their worship, is also accepted by millions of other Christians as a testimony of their faith—Episcopalians, Presbyterians, Methodists, Lutherans, and members of many of the Reformed Churches.[1] In fact, an international committee, representing nine major Protestant churches and Roman Catholicism, have recently approved an English translation of both the *Gloria* and the *Creed,* to be used in all their churches.

It might be useful to reproduce here the full text of this Protestant-Catholic translation of the Nicene Creed, if only in order to remind ourselves that it represents, in its antiquity, the profession of faith of the Christian Church before its many divisions into Eastern Orthodox and Protestant denominations:

> We believe in one God, almighty Father,
>   maker of heaven and earth,
>   and of all things visible and invisible.

[1] *Editor's note:* Many of these Protestant groups which recognize the Nicene Creed ordinarily use the briefer Apostles' Creed in their services. There is wide agreement, however, among non-Catholic theological scholars that the Nicene Creed has occupied a crucial place in the statement of those basic beliefs about Jesus Christ that are shared by Catholic and non-Catholic Christians.

We believe in the one Lord, Jesus Christ, the only Son of God,
    begotten of the Father from all eternity:
    God from God, Light from Light, true God from true God:
    begotten, not made, one in being with the Father.
Through him all things were made.
For us men and for our salvation he came down from
    heaven.
By the power of the Holy Spirit
    he was born of the Virgin Mary and became Man.
He was crucified for us under Pontius Pilate;
    he suffered, died and was buried. He arose on the third day
    in accordance with the scriptures.
He entered into heaven and is seated
    at the right hand of the Father.
We believe in the Holy Spirit, the Lord, the giver of life,
    who proceeds from the Father and the Son.
Together with the Father and the Son
    he is adored and glorified.
He has spoken through the prophets.
We believe in one, holy, catholic, and apostolic Church.
We acknowledge one baptism for the forgiveness of sins.
We look for the resurrection of the dead
    and the life of the world to come.   Amen.

Having made its profession of faith in the Triune God, and
having affirmed its belief in the great events which God wrought
in His Son, among men while being Himself a Man, the wor-
shiping assembly now moves toward the offering of God to God.
The bread and wine are brought to the altar, symbolizing, as did
the sacrifices of the Old Testament, man's return to the Creator
of the gifts needed to sustain life which He had produced from
the earth for the feeding of His children. These gifts, stained with
all the imperfections and weakness of man, but blessed with his
desire to at least *desire* to love and serve the Father, are placed
upon the altar in anticipation of God's response to man's gift.

After recalling God's many mercies to man, and after having
invoked His blessing upon the Church throughout the world, those

present in the assembly, and all mankind, the priest-celebrant then "reminds" God the Father that all of this has been done, not only in the memory, but in the Name of His Son, "Who the night before He suffered, took bread, blessed it broke and gave to his disciples saying, 'This is My Body; Take and eat of It, all of you.' And when supper was ended He took the wine, blessed it and gave it to them, saying, 'This is My Blood of the New Covenant; take and drink It, all of you.' "

For the Roman Catholic, these words whereby the priest consecrates the bread and wine into the Body and Blood of Christ have meaning only because the human priest stands at the altar table in the name and by the authority of Christ, the Great High Priest.

This, in the Roman Catholic understanding, is precisely the understanding of the early Church as its Eucharistic practice was recorded in the Epistles of Paul the Apostle and Peter, as well as in the Acts of the Apostles. Peter himself might, perhaps, not fully understand all that was going on if he were to attend a "solemn Mass" in St. Peter's Basilica in Rome, or if he were to drop in on a "folk Mass" accompanied by guitar twanging and rock-rhythm singing at a Catholic Mass for young people. But he would surely recognize the words of Consecration uttered by the priest, and would have joined in the reverent hush which embraces the congregation at this point in the Mass.

The thrust of the prayers after the Consecration is to recall, in the presence of God, the memory of the great things which have been wrought by God for man—in much the same way that the Jewish Passover meal recalls to those at table God's outstretched arms of mercy and love in the events of the Exodus, the passage through the Sea of Reeds, and the journey through the desert toward the land which He had promised.

This portion of the Mass is called the *Anamnesis*—the remembering. This remembering is common to many Protestant celebrations of the Lord's Supper, even as it has been retained in the liturgy of the Eastern Orthodox Churches. The Orthodox

Churches, however, have retained in their liturgies something which had all but vanished from most liturgies of Western Christianity: the *Epiclesis*—the summoning of the Holy Spirit, whom Christ had promised on the occasion of the first Eucharistic Banquet.

Fortunately, but very belatedly, Roman Catholicism has become aware of its general neglect of the Holy Spirit. One feels reassured that the Holy Spirit has not in turn neglected the Church, and feels that the Second Vatican Council and its aftermath give evidence that the Spirit is breathing anew throughout the Church, even in places where some people would prefer that He take His influence elsewhere. At any rate, recent revisions in the celebration of the Eucharist do make explicit, within the Roman Catholic liturgy, this ancient invitation to the Spirit, Who in the words of a medieval hymn cited earlier, "straightens what has become bent, makes shine again that which had become rusted, and makes green once more the earth which had become parched and barren."

The entire assembly, priest and people, now join in the recitation of the Lord's Prayer. Here, too, we see the effort, made through changes in the liturgy, to deepen the awareness of the worshipers that the Mass is an act of the community.

Until several years ago, the priest recited the Our Father in Latin, and the congregation responded "Amen." This liturgical custom illustrates very graphically how far removed the liturgy in its practice had become from what its theory actually was. Our Lord, in giving us this prayer, had specifically enjoined Christians, "When you pray, pray thus—." Our Lord also gave us this prayer in the language which He and his hearers used, Aramaic. It was, therefore, a prayer, composed by Our Lord Himself, recited in the language of the people. Yet in the liturgy of the Roman Church, the priest, not the people, recited this prayer, and in a language which had not been the language of any people for centuries.

After the Our Father, priest and people say prayers of preparation for the reception of Holy Communion. After the priest has taken both the Body and the Blood, he moves to the edge of the Sanctuary to give a Consecrated Host, the Body, to those who wish to receive. Again, we must note a recent change. Roman Catholics had not received both the bread and the wine since the late Middle Ages. Now, however, the laity can receive both the bread and the wine at the Mass which accompanies their marriage, on the anniversary of their marriage, or at Masses celebrated for special occasions. There is a growing tendency for priests to interpret "special occasions" quite broadly, so that Holy Communion, in the form of both bread and wine, is in many places of the country administered even when Catholics have gathered for study groups or conventions. It is, of course, only a conjecture, but I would think that the laity, at least in the United States, will within the space of five years be receiving the Body and the Blood even at regular Sunday Masses in their parishes.

The Roman Catholic has always believed, of course, that in receiving only the Consecrated Bread he was also receiving the Consecrated Wine; since he believed that he was receiving the Living Christ—as really present within him as within the womb of Mary—then it was obvious that this totally present, Living Christ came with both Body and Blood, since the one cannot be conceived as living without the other.

For the Roman Catholic, then, Holy Communion means his encounter, not only with Jesus Christ, "the same, yesterday, today, and for ever," but also with the Father and the Holy Spirit. The Catholic conceives this encounter quite literally: he, a human person, is meeting the Divine Person. It is this emphasis upon the person, and the rich meaning of the encounter between a human being and God, that makes the reception of the Eucharist perhaps the most meaningful religious experience in the life of the Roman Catholic. I am aware, of course, that many if not most Protestants emphasize the importance in their religion of experience, particularly the experience of "meeting Christ." For the Catholic, such an experience is not rare; it is not an intensely dramatic moment, a once-and-for-all thing. I can encounter Christ, His Father and His Spirit weekly in the Mass and through Holy Communion; indeed, I can meet the Triune God daily in my Church if I choose because wherever circumstances permit Mass is offered daily.

The Catholic also sees, as has been mentioned above, that Mass and Holy Communion sum up, as it were, all of his theology and religious thinking. For faith is not exclusively, or even primarily, an assent of the mind to truths about God as embodied in the Nicene Creed. Faith is less an *assent* of the mind than it is a *consent* of the entire being—my effort, at least, to say yes to an invading God Who comes bearing a sword both to my unruly flesh and my stubborn spirit and yet, paradoxically, through the two-edged sword brings peace.

For many Protestants, the experience of God would seem to be primarily an individual one: "God and I have encountered one another." For the Catholic, however, the experience of God in Holy Communion is—or certainly should be—not only individual, but communal. God has not come to me in this ineffably intimate way as a reward for my virtues, or as a comfort in my fears and anxieties. He has come to strengthen me for His own uses; I have received Him as a member of a Church, whose mission it is "to proclaim deliverance to the captive, to preach the Gospel to the poor, to bring light to those who are blind."

How can I pretend that I have received the Triune God in Holy Communion if the reception of Communion turns me inward, in rapt contemplation of the state of my own soul? Once I have admitted Christ so fully into my being, I must also through the same door admit all of that motley crowd whom He insists on bringing with Him, and to whom He seems to reserve special love: the poor, the outcast, the publicans, the sinners.

How, lastly, can I pretend that I have spoken to and heard the Triune God unless, when I leave the sanctuary for the street, I also have had my ears attuned to the cries of distress and anguish that come from the starving and the war-afflicted half a world away, or to the sobs that come from the home of a neighbor or even, perhaps, from within my own home.

The reception of Holy Communion, then, is paradoxical: it is an intensely individual and deeply personal experience, wherein even more intimately than Moses one ascends the mountain and meets his God. He has, however, met God in the Presence of His family. The Eucharist is, as we have pointed out, a sacred family meal, a sacrificial banquet. Through the fellowship of the broken Body and shed Blood, I am drawn more tightly, with the iron bonds of love, not only to the members of my family who share my faith, but I am also driven by divine command into greater love and sacrificial service of the entire family of man, who are, like me, sons of God and adopted brothers of Jesus Christ.

After the Eucharist has been distributed, the priest-celebrant returns to the altar, cleanses the vessels which had been used, and then, together with the people, prays that the grace and strength given by God may not be lost through the indifference and weakness of man. Priest and people then join in a recessional hymn and the congregation moves to its other concerns for that day—a visit to or from the in-laws, witnessing a sports event either at the field or on TV, doing homework, mowing the lawn. It is the intention of the Church that whatever is done will be done in a somewhat different, immeasurably heightened way because whatever is done could be done with Christ acting in and through the human agent with whom He has honored the Father, and to whom He has come as He once came to fishermen-brothers on a shore, and changed their lives.

What we have just attempted to describe as being the heart of a Roman Catholic Mass can, of course, take place in a complex variety of circumstances. A Solemn High Midnight Mass nationally telecast from St. Patrick's Cathedral in New York City will, in many ways, look quite different from a Mass celebrated in a high school or college classroom, or in the home of a Roman Catholic. The last circumstance is worth noting, because the Catholic Church, which had once surrounded the celebration of the Mass with a thick hedge of prescriptions and prohibitions, now permits Mass to be celebrated within the home, and permission to have such a Mass is rather easy to obtain in almost every diocese in the United States. The reason, of course, is obvious: the Mass is for the people, and the locale and liturgy which make the sacrificial banquet most meaningful for a given sector of the people of God can be determined by the people as well as by bishops, including the Bishop of Rome.

Perhaps all that need be said on the question of home Masses is that Peter, the first bishop of Rome, would have felt perfectly at home participating in one of them.

As we turn to leave the "Dining Room" wherein the Mass has been celebrated, we notice in a corner of the room a small knot of people. There are youngsters, seemingly brothers and sisters, assorted adults and, in the center of the group, standing near a font of water, is a woman holding a baby in her arms. A priest is pouring a slight amount of water on the baby's forehead and we can hear the words, "I baptize thee in the name of the Father and of the Son and of the Holy Spirit."

The fact that the Roman Catholic Church, along with a number of Protestant Churches, practices the Baptism of infants strikes other Christians as strange, and we should, therefore, pause just a moment to consider what we are witnessing.

Whole forests have been turned into wood pulp to make the paper on which the Christian controversy over infant Baptism has been written. Obviously, we could not begin even to summarize in these pages the origin, development, and present state of this controversy. Our purpose here, then, will not be to defend the Roman Catholic practice of infant Baptism, but simply to explain why the Roman Catholic Church baptizes infants. For the Roman Catholic, following St. Paul, Baptism is the means whereby a person enters the Church. Another, and perhaps more significant way of expressing the same reality, is to say that through Baptism one becomes a member of the Body of Christ, is "grafted onto Christ." It will be recognized that these metaphors, too, are from Paul the Apostle.

These last two metaphors indicate the notion, not of an individual deciding to join a club, but of a living community welcoming a new member. Although no one, including the Pope, can baptize against his will anyone who has reached the age of reason, the Church nonetheless baptizes an infant, who cannot but be totally oblivious to what is being done to him and in his name. Why?

Precisely because being incorporated into Christ is so important, the Church feels that the newborn, who has just received the gift of life, should also begin to live with this deeper life which is Christ as soon as possible after the infant's entry upon this uncertain, whirling planet. Faith, in this instance, will follow Baptism rather than Baptism's following faith, as is the case with those who have reached the age where decision is possible. The infant cannot "choose Christ" but Christ has already chosen the infant, through the circumstances of the child's being born of Christian parents who consider the Baptism of their child a matter of utmost importance.

According to psychologists and sociologists, one of the major problems which a human being encounters in his passing through life is that of being accepted as a person, a "someone" rather than an it, a "something." Through Baptism, even at the very beginning of life, the infant becomes a someone. He receives a name—his Christian name—which will be his through both time and eternity. He has already become a person with a name within the Christian community, which has not only received him but has contracted obligations and responsibilities toward him. These include assuring him that he will receive from the community the means of growing in the knowledge and love of God if he chooses to avail himself of what the community places at his disposal.

The redemptive death of Christ on Calvary is already effective for the infant, even before his Baptism—just as that redemptive death is effective for those who have never known or never will know Jesus Christ, or have His Gospel preached to them. For according to Catholic belief, Jesus died to save all men, and they will be saved, even without their knowing why, so long as they live by their conscience. Baptism for the infant, then, does not mean his having Christ's death made effective for him by the pouring of water upon his forehead, nor through the promises of fidelity to Christ made in his name by his sponsors at Baptism. Baptism, for the infant, means that he has entered into the community of the Faith, and has been incorporated into Christ. He may, obviously, at a future date knowingly renounce the promise made in his name, and reject his union with Christ, even as any Christian capable of sin may choose a creature rather than his Creator, prefer his own will to God's will. Again, obviously, the person grafted on to Christ at infancy must himself later, over and over again, choose to remain so grafted.

Infant Baptism, then, represents not a distinctively different view of Baptism from that of the churches which do not practice it, but represents simply a different emphasis. So important, in the Catholic view, is incorporation into the Body of Christ that where conscious faith, as in the case of the infant, cannot precede Baptism, then Baptism should precede faith.

It is for this reason, among others, that the Roman Catholic Church, unlike most Protestant Churches, has retained its understanding of Confirmation as a Sacrament—a visible sign both indicating and bestowing God's merciful love, i.e., grace.

Although the precise scriptural justifications are debatable, it seems clear that the early Church did practice a rite which the Catholic Church, along with a few Protestant communities, calls Confirmation.

This rite, which involved anointing the baptized Christian with consecrated oil, was seen as a completion of the grace-filled ceremonies which brought a person into the household of the Faith. In this ancient view, the Sacrament of Confirmation (reenforcement) makes of those who receive it complete Christians.

Confirmation, then, as many texts long before the Reformation point out, is the Sacrament of Christian maturity. It assumes that the baptized person who receives it wishes to receive it. It therefore embraces those persons entering adolescence who have had an opportunity to grow within, and test their allegiance to, the Christian community which had warmly accepted them at Baptism.

It is possible, and valid, to compare the Sacrament of Confirmation with the Jewish liturgical practice of the Bar Mitzva, whereby one becomes the son of the Covenant. It is also possible, and valid, to compare the Sacrament of Confirmation with the initiation rites which we now know to take place when a boy approaching young adulthood is formally admitted into the tribe in a ceremony which declares to him both what he has a right to expect from the tribe and the responsibility of his contribution to the tribe.

I would wish, however, to bypass both of these possible similarities to the Sacrament of Confirmation, and to consider briefly a similarity much more relevant: the fact that the Sacrament of Confirmation, in the Roman Catholic and Eastern Orthodox understanding, is very close to the ritualistic meaning of Baptism in those Christian Churches which either do not permit or do not favor the Baptism of infants.

Whereas, in the case of one baptized in infancy no promises of faith could be expected, a confession of conscious faith is required of candidates for Confirmation. Further, they are expected to have had, at least in possibility, an experience of having encountered the Triune God within the community of faith—an experience which would empower them to wish to seal this encounter with a pledge of their own fidelity to the God Who had already shown Himself faithful to them.

The actual practice of the Roman Catholic Church with regard to the administration of Confirmation has varied almost as wildly as a wind vane in a hurricane. Despite these differences, determined by different times and shifting circumstances, the basic understanding of the Church has remained the same. Confirmation completes the entrance into the Church, the grafting of the individual into the tree of Christ which had begun at Baptism. The one confirmed is also anointed with *chrism*—an oil—in close memory of the oil used, in Old Testament times, for the consecration of both priests and kings.

The young Christian who has thus been anointed is to stand within the Christian community with the function both of priestly mediation and sacrifice, and the kingly function of ruling others in the only sense that ruling has within the Christian understanding of the term: to rule others is to serve them.

Confirmation thus becomes, at least within Roman Catholicism, the Sacrament of adulthood; it completes the process begun at Baptism, even as the growth toward maturity represents a development of the infant into man. In this sense, since it places such heavy emphasis on the choice of the one confirmed fully and consciously to be a follower of Christ, it absorbs within itself many of the religious understandings which surround Baptism in those Christian communities which baptize only the young adult or the adult. Like Baptism, Confirmation is once and for all; it is not to be repeated, because it represents a definitive orientation of the one confirmed to Christ. Like Baptism, moreover, it is a Sacrament which, while affecting the individual, takes place within a community of faith. It therefore represents not only the completely voluntary decision of the one confirmed to enter an assembly of believers, the Church, but also betokens the community's acceptance of the individual.

Confirmation is, therefore, essentially a Sacrament of Pentecost. It will be recalled that on the occasion of the first Pentecost, so far as the New Testament reveals, the Apostles huddled in fear in the Upper Room had received only the Baptism of John. Christ had promised to them a Baptism, not with water alone, but with the Holy Spirit, which the Apostles were to receive not many days after His Ascension (Acts 1:5).

The first Christians, then, were baptized amid the Wind and Fire of Pentecost. The work which Christ had begun in them was completed by His sending of the promised Spirit.

It is here, perhaps, that one can see another, very important similarity between the Roman Catholic understanding of Confirmation as a Sacrament and the practice of adult or near-adult Baptism in other Churches. The Roman Catholic Church is often questioned (and not without reason) for its seeming neglect of a theology of the Holy Spirit. Confirmation, however, gives the basis of such a theology even though, for complex historical reasons, Catholicism has often failed, over long periods of time, to explore and explain this theology. The Church's teaching has always been, however, that through the Sacrament of Confirmation not only is the Holy Spirit imparted to the one confirmed, but that the Spirit leaves within the individual His distinctive gifts. These are gifts given directly by the Spirit to the individual; they do not come to him intermediately through either the bishop or the priest; the gifts are not received, like mail in war time marked "Censored and Approved." Wisdom, knowledge, understanding, counsel, fortitude, piety, fear of the Lord—these gifts belong completely to the individual and are imparted to him with a shape and purpose as distinctively his as the shape of his nose or the slant of his handwriting. The fact that each individual within the Church has received the staggeringly magnificent gifts of the Holy Spirit as his own underlies the Church's newly recovered understanding of the role of the lay person within the Church—a role which we will consider in greater detail in a subsequent chapter.

It has been indicated, several times before, that the Roman Catholic Church rests, in effect, upon a sacramental system. Not all of these Sacraments find their full setting within the Dining Room, the "Chapel," and we have perhaps been long enough within this room in any case. Before we open the doors to leave, however, I must warn you, I fear, that what we may see and hear outside these doors might be rather turbulent and noisy, certainly confusing, and perhaps scandalous. I am taking a deep breath, and suggest that you do likewise.

5

The Main Hall

As I had warned you, the scene *is* noisy and confusing. We may, indeed, occasionally have to raise our voices in order to be heard. As I attempt to guide you through this section of the house, it may be necessary from time to time to ask you to be careful, lest you be poked in the eye by a picket sign carried by a priest, layman, or nun.

This hall was once very serene. The tone was one of almost reverent hush as people came and went about their business. The bishops have their offices on the second floor, and people ascended and descended the stairs with a consciousness that they were in the presence of power—rather paternalistic power and often very beneficient power, but power nonetheless. The Papal offices occupy the third floor, but very few ever got that far. The hall, in its tasteful appointments, in its rather ancient furnishings, in its hushed atmosphere, suggested a palace.

Now, as you can see, all this is changed. There are excited comings and goings, and considerable loud talking and shouting. Some priests, nuns, and lay people are holding a sit-in on the stairs, and the bishops frequently have trouble stepping over protestors as they negotiate the way to or from their offices. Occasionally, a voice can be heard coming from the third floor asking in patient, weary tones if the people on the floors below could not possibly manage to be less noisy and obstreperous.

So far as the Roman Catholic Church in America is concerned, the present conflict between "freedom and authority" can be epitomized in what took place in Washington, D.C., during the week of November 11 to 15, 1968, when the American bishops held their semiannual meeting. As these 235 bishops assembled in Washington, they found themselves the target of a most unusual and quite bizarre series of demonstrations by dissident priests and unhappy lay people. Cardinal O'Boyle of Washington had, some weeks before, disciplined forty-one of his Washington priests because they had criticized Pope Paul's encyclical on birth control, *Humanae Vitae.* In the next chapter we shall return to Pope Paul, the question of papal infallibility, and the question of birth control. For the moment we are concerned with what is happening to those who, like Cardinal O'Boyle, assert their authority as bishops to reprimand priests who feel that they cannot accept the encyclical, and the reaction of such priests and laymen who share their views. We are concerned, then, at this point not with the question of Papal infallibility, but with the clash between the forces of authority and the forces supporting "freedom" within the Church.

The day before the American bishops assembled, a rally was held in Washington. More than three thousand Catholic lay people crowded into the Mayflower Hotel to demonstrate their support of the disciplined priests and their opposition to Cardinal O'Boyle. The keynote speaker for this rally was one of the nation's best-known Catholic laymen, Senator Eugene McCarthy, who had been a strong candidate for the Democratic presidential nomination and had, as a young man, been a novice in a Benedictine monastery. Senator McCarthy opened his remarks by noting that he had not come to the rally "either to establish a third party or a second Church."

His mere reference to a second Church touched on a situation which many fear, or hope, might develop within Roman Catholicism: a schism, a split between those who emphasize authority and those who insist upon freedom. This "silent schism," as some call it, already exists within the Church, certainly within American Catholicism. It was demonstrated, again during that week in Washington, when 140 priests came to the lobby of the hotel where the bishops were meeting and staged a sit-in in support of the priests who had been censured by Cardinal O'Boyle.

Not to be outdone by the priests in this display of a new kind of pressure to be applied to bishops, the next night 120 lay people came to the same hotel and demonstrated for two hours. They prayed that the disciplined priests would be granted "due process" in their dispute with Cardinal O'Boyle—and also prayed for "the proper use of authority in the Church." They also sang, symbolically enough, "The Battle Hymn of the Republic" and "The Impossible Dream."

What, indeed, has happened to the Church? Why has it seemed suddenly to be transformed from a huge, smoothly working ecclesiastical machine into a "an institutional shambles," as a famous Protestant theologian described it in talking to me the week after Washington? Has the Catholic Church become indeed "a house divided"? The last is, of course, a very real possibility, and I would not wish even to run the risk of minimizing this possibility.

I think, however, that the present situation within the Church, resulting from a head-on confrontation between authority and freedom, is better represented, not by the metaphor of "a house divided," but by a more commonplace image. An undeservedly anonymous bard once wrote:

> There was a dachshund once, so long
> He hadn't any notion
> How long it took to notify
> His tail of his emotion.
> And so it happened, while his eyes
> Were filled with woe and sadness
> His little tail went wagging on
> Because of previous gladness.

It may seem far-fetched to note in the emotionally-divided dachshund an analogue to the operation of authority within the postconciliar Church, but I, for one, can't get that dachshund from my mind when I pick up the papers these days.

One reads of priests being "silenced" in a number of dioceses other than Washington, D.C., and in other dioceses one reads of priests writing to Rome to have their archbishop involuntarily retired. In many dioceses within the United States, the bishops are making heroic efforts to structure a dialogue with their people— priests, nuns, and laity—and yet in other dioceses, wherein the bishop rules like a descendant of the Medicis, his chancery, his episcopal headquarters, resembles a besieged citadel, with pickets marching around it like Joshua's legions before Jericho.

Before the Second Vatican Council, such things never were; had the Council not been so revolutionary, such things would not have been. But the Council was, and these things are and will be, so long as some people holding authority and some people subject to authority remain confused about the nature and proper exercise of authority within the Church.

If Catholics themselves are confused by this new approach to authority in the Church, what must be the state of mind of the Protestant? I am not at all sure that I can make clear what is happening, but I must make the effort. The shouting, the mutual recriminations, the folk songs and sit-ins are merely symptoms of this confusion. In themselves, they do not provide much clarification of the point at issue: the meaning of authority in the Church, and its relation to the freedom of those within the Church. I would suggest that we try to find a quiet corner somewhere and attempt to discuss what the Second Vatican Council did say about authority, and contrast this to the older view of authority which had dominated Catholic thinking.

As you are already aware, the Council made considerable changes within certain structures of Roman Catholicism—structures dealing with what might be called "ecclesiastical administration." Thus the Council itself was a demonstration of collegiality. After Vatican Council I, with its definition of Papal infallibility, it had been thought by many within and without Roman Catholicism that there need be indeed through the long future no subsequent Council. The summoning of the Second Vatican Council, therefore, in itself was a demonstration of collegiality and the assembled fathers, the bishops of the Council, laid great stress upon their collegial exercise of authority together with the Pope.

Following the Council, there has been the creation of the international Synod of Bishops, most of them elected from within their own national bodies. There has also been, since the Council, the creation in most countries of national synods of bishops, acting with greater autonomy and authority than had been the case in the past. In many dioceses within the United States there has been the creation of diocesan senates, consisting of elected priests and lay people, something quite new to American Catholicism.

At the present time, in more than half of the Roman Catholic dioceses in the United States, there are also priest senates, bodies consisting of priests who have been elected by their fellow priests to serve as advisory and administrative arms and agents of the bishops. All of these developments would certainly seem to indicate an increasing democratization, we might call it, within Roman Catholicism. I feel it quite safe to say that the overwhelming majority of American Catholics—bishops, priests, and laity—welcome the introduction of these democratic structures and the inauguration of such democratic processes.

I would, however, like to point out (as I have had occasion to point out to groups of Roman Catholics, particularly priests) that far more important for the life of the Church than democratic processes is the assurance of *democratic values;* and democratic values, as we know from our own political history, are not always necessarily preserved by democratic processes and structures.

The key values to be preserved in the democratization of the church I would take to be analogous to the key values within a political democracy. And I would take it that the key values of democracy are that it allows a human being to participate communally in a humanizing endeavor by which he becomes more free. It thus makes possible his sharing in the major decisions which will affect his life within the community.

It is for this reason, for example, that democracy, at least as we understand it, involves such inseparable and nonnegotiable features as freedom of the press, freedom of speech, freedom of assembly, and freedom of petition for the redress of wrongs. It is against this background, then, of democratic values, rather than exclusively a concern with democratic processes, that I should like to discuss the increasing democratization within the Roman Catholic Church after the Council, particularly in terms of the new relationships established between hierarchy, clergy, and laity.

The Second Vatican Council in the area of these relationships, as in so many other areas, established new frontiers. It was characteristic of the Second Vatican Council that it was not *dogmatic,* as so many previous Councils had perforce been. Nor did it set out in every case the theology which underlies so many of its statements. There are, however in the conciliar statements on the role of the bishop, conceived primarily as that of pastor, on the role of the clergy, and the role of the laity, theological presuppositions which will engage the attention of the theologians within Catholicism for some time to come.

For the purpose of our visiting together I would extract but one consideration—namely, the understanding in the documents of the Council of the Church as the people of God—a *koinonia,* a community—called together by Christ and in Christ. The Council here makes an extremely significant statement when it says that all the members of this divinely summoned *koinonia,* all the members of the people of God, are alike summoned to sanctity, called to holiness. Each of the members, therefore, is called to *grow into the fulness of Christ,* which means in effect that there are, within the Church, this people of God on pilgrimage, not degrees of citizenship, but only differences of function and varieties of responsibility. The Council also points out that every Roman Catholic has at the heart of his calling the responsibility of *diakonia*—service to his fellowman, because it is only through serving my fellowman that I can serve God.

Koinonia, community, and *diakonia,* the vocation of service— these are the foundations upon which the Church is built. Authority in the Church exists to support community and service; community and service do not exist in the Church to serve authority. This, at any rate, is the understanding of the role of authority in the Church in the documents of the Second Vatican Council— even though many people in the Church, laity as well as priests and bishops, seem to feel frightened by the new and prefer the older understanding of authority.

The Second Vatican Council introduced, if not a new, at least a recovered and restored understanding of authority within the Church, an understanding rather sharply opposed to what had been for centuries the previous understanding of such authority. I think if we have to draw a diagram of the way in which authority in the Church had been previously understood by most Roman Catholics, the diagram we would come up with would be that of a triangle, or perhaps a pyramid. The summit of authority, the apex of the pyramid, would, of course, be the Roman Pontiff, regarded by Roman Catholics as the Vicar of Christ. Then from him authority would descend vertically to the next stratum of the pyramid, the Pope's fellow bishops throughout the world. Authority would come down from that stratum to the next, the clergy. Those next in authority, considered always descending in this vertical line, would perhaps be the religious men and women, the nuns and members of religious orders. Forming the broad, inert base of the pyramid, in fact supporting the heavy weight of all above it, would be the stratum of the laity.

Given this understanding, or at least this thought-model of authority, it was almost inevitable, I suppose, that we Roman Catholics would then set about constructing other pyramids on the model of the large pyramid. In the parish, for example, the structure of authority would again be considered a pyramid, with the pastor at the apex, his curates forming the next stratum; the stratum beneath that, the nuns or brothers who taught in the parochial school; lastly, again forming the broad base, contributing funds and children to the school and to the church, came the laity.

Even when it came to the question of authority within the Catholic family, we Catholics tended to follow the thought pattern of the pyramid. The Catholic family itself became a *pyramidunculus,* a tiny pyramid, with the apex being the father, who exercised (or was permitted to think he exercised) the ultimate authority; the next stratum his wife, forming a buffer between him and the broad base of the pyramid—the children and their assorted pets.

This understanding of authority, which did mark almost every area in which Christian authority was exercised within the Church, is obviously monarchical, and would seem to have been borrowed from a political model which slowly evolved through the centuries from the time of Constantine.

The Council reintroduced another understanding of authority, as we have indicated. But, there is reason to fear that even at the present moment this new understanding of authority is but little understood by most Roman Catholics, including a number of Roman Catholics who wield considerable authority. It would be in an effort, then, to shed some light upon this newer understanding of authority that I would suggest that we Roman Catholics, in order to deepen our understanding and assuage some of our fears, might turn away from political models, including that of democracy. For an understanding of authority, I suggest that we turn not to political structures, but instead to what sociologists have told us about the way in which authority, any authority, is most effectively exercised within a community.

Sociologists, as you know, have made studies of rather complex organizations, such as the German *Wehrmacht* and the American military establishment, and a number of large American super corporations. The findings of these sociologists are extremely interesting, and deserve the most careful consideration from Roman Catholics. The sociologists have filtered out the conclusion that anyone who holds ultimate authority, and therefore responsibility, within a given community, cannot, properly speaking, be said to have even begun to exercise his authority when he has arrived at a policy decision. The exercise of his authority begins, say the sociologists, only when the one holding ultimate authority has begun to enlist the voluntary cooperation of those who have to carry out his decisions.

Secondly, the sociologists point out, the making of decisions on the part of the one holding ultimate authority, and therefore responsibility, should not be the lonely exercise that many Roman Catholics long thought it necessarily had to be. Rather, the one holding ultimate authority should try to involve as many people in the organization—the community—as he possibly can in the process of decision-making. The sociologists are pointing out, in effect, that the one who holds authority, even in a large, extremely complex organization, should reach out to involve as many members as possible; first, in the decision-making, and second, once the decision has been made, in winning their voluntary cooperation in implementing the decision communally arrived at.

Thirdly, the sociologists point out, the one holding this ultimate authority should give every possible freedom to those who are entrusted with carrying out the decision which has been made. Putting it in other terms, we might say that what the sociologists are recommending is that the one in authority be genuinely in a position to say to those under his authority, not *fiat,* "let it be done," but *faciamus,* "let us do this together."

It is important for Roman Catholics to realize that the sociologists who have made these analyses of authority in a variety of complex organizations are not discussing the nature or the source of such authority. They are simply talking about the way in which authority is most effectively exercised. They are not suggesting that those who are to hold authority be elected by those who will be subject to authority. They have not suggested, for example, as a result of their analyses, that the employees elect the president of General Motors, or that the noncommissioned officers elect the members of the General Staff. To repeat, they are not discussing the nature or the source of authority. They *are* discussing the most effective mode of exercising authority. An aspect of this becomes, I think, rather interesting. One of the sociologists has said that to coin a term describing this best way of exercising authority, we perhaps would not come upon a better one than *familial authority*. Remember, of course, that we are discussing a family of adults.

To the Roman Catholic, the findings of the sociologists should not, certainly, appear novel or strange or dangerous. They are simply recommending for large corporations and the military a *mode* of authority with which Roman Catholics should have been quite familiar, at least in theory. For this is precisely the way in which authority was to have been exercised in the tradition of the Roman Catholic religious orders and communities. Consider the example of St. Ignatius Loyola, the founder of the Jesuits. Though many consider this order to be quasi military, Loyola said that it is the Holy Spirit Himself, rather than written laws and constitutions, which are to guide the Jesuits to the goals of the community.

Centuries before Ignatius Loyola there was the great figure of St. Benedict, in so many ways the source and fountainhead of the Roman Catholic tradition of religious community. He wrote that the abbot of a Benedictine community should be like a father toward his subjects. But there is no suggestion in the rules of St. Benedict of the kind of paternalism which has afflicted, in fact, so many Roman Catholic religious orders in the past and which has indeed at times afflicted the entire Roman Catholic body. St. Benedict, for example, pointed out that the abbot, in arriving at decisions affecting the entire monastery, should discuss the problems with *all* the members of the monastery. And then he went on to say that the abbot should be careful to pay attention to even the youngest novice in the community. Why? Because, Benedict continued, *the Holy Spirit might be speaking to the abbot through even the youngest novice.* This is what I suppose in current sociological terms we would mean by an open community— although obviously, for the abbot, it represented something like a mine field.

And yet, the real source of the Roman Catholic theoretic understanding and familiarity with authority goes obviously beyond St. Benedict to the words and example of Christ Himself in his relationship to His community. "I will not call you servants, but friends." When there was discussion, you will recall, as to who was to be the greatest among the apostles, Christ presented the child as the example of the one greatest in the community. In that tremendously moving moment at the Last Supper, when again there was jockeying for position among the Apostles, Christ washed their feet and enjoined on them the imitation of his act. "You call me Lord, and so I am. But if I have washed your feet, wash you one another's feet." This, then, is the mark of authority, as the Vatican Council has stressed. This is the mark of authority within the Catholic, indeed, within any Christian community; that authority exists for service. The vocation of every Christian is to be of service, and therefore he who holds authority is to be the servant of the servant. Authority, then, within such a community does not mean primarily the power to command or coerce. Authority is primarily for service.

There is an interesting etymological facet to the word "authority"; when we trace it back to its roots, it seems to involve the Latin word *augeo,* meaning "to grow." The task of one holding authority in a Christian community is the task, then, of assisting the members of that community to grow. When we discuss the question of authority within Roman Catholicism, we tend to think almost exclusively of the tension between the bishop and his people, of the tension between a pastor and his parishioners, and so on. Yet, actually, what we have just been attempting to say applies to Christian authority wherever it is to be found.

It applies, for example, to the authority exercised by a Christian teacher within a classroom. The primary responsibility of such a teacher is to help those taught toward growth. The same understanding, and therefore responsibility, is to be found in the authority which I, for example, exercise within my family. My primary responsibility as one holding authority in a Christian family is to assist the members of my family, my wife and my children, to grow in Christ. Not primarily to demand nor to coerce, in the case of the children, but to assist in growth. And this is the thrust that gets closest to the bone. I am expected to do this not nearly so much by what I say as by what I am. Unless, then, I use my parental authority to serve, unless I use it for my children's growth, then I have not exercised the authority of Christian parenthood at all.

In considering, in short, the nature of authority in the Church, the Second Vatican Council obviously centered on the nature of authority, not for command or coercion, but for service. It also stressed that policy-shaping and decision-making within the Church were to be "collegial"—and we have attempted to show that collegial decision-making is precisely the type of exercise of authority which contemporary sociologists have found most effective, even in large corporations. Lastly, the Council strongly urged that structures for such collegial exercise of authority be instituted on every level of the Church's life: not only in dioceses, but also in individual parishes, and should also be reflected in the way in which Christian authority is exercised within the school and within the home. The Pope and the bishops, assembled in Rome, did quite well on the subject of authority in the session of the Vatican Council which ended in December, 1965. Let us return, however, to Washington, D.C., where the American bishops were meeting in November, 1968.

A small news story coming out of Washington in the week of the bishop's meeting has about it a touch of pathos, but also a note of somber significance. In October, 1968, fifty-one priests of the Archdiocese of San Antonio, Texas, had revealed that they had written more than a month before to Pope Paul urging him to ask for the retirement of their seventy-seven-year-old archbishop. Several years before, Pope Paul had himself suggested that bishops request retirement when they had reached the age of seventy-five. The Archbishop of San Antonio had not volunteered his resignation, nor had it been requested by the Vatican. In the opinion of the priests signing the letter, at least, their archbishop was exercising his authority over them in an arbitrary manner, quite contrary to the prescriptions of the Second Vatican Council.

In response to the priests' making their letter public, as they had told the Vatican they would if no answer were forthcoming within thirty days, the Archbishop of San Antonio reacted strongly. The offending priests were, in many cases, removed from their positions. Little, if any, effort was made to initiate a genuine dialogue between the prelate and his priests.

Such action by a bishop could, at one time, have been done under the cloak of silence; the fact that the priests had written would have been kept secret; the fact that the Vatican did not answer would have been kept secret; the archbishop's punitive action would have been kept secret. Those days, as everyone knows with the seeming exception of certain bishops, are gone forever.

When the news of all this was made public in the press, many laymen and women in San Antonio gave public support to the priests through public meetings which spotlighted this particular instance of a conflict over authority. A group of lay people in San Antonio gathered 4,750 signatures on a petition urging the retirement of their archbishop.

One of these laymen, Samuel Snell, who operates a chain of beauty shops in San Antonio, was delegated to present this petition to the American bishops during their Washington assembly. Unable to find any official of the National Conference of Catholic bishops to receive the petition, he stared into a cup of coffee and, according to the press dispatch, said bitterly: "The Vatican Council told me that as a responsible layman I have views that should be expressed and that I should do this through channels. Well, that's what I'm here to do, but I can't even find the damn channels."

The bishops, themselves, seemed also to be having trouble finding or creating channels which would enable them to act together, as the Vatican Council had urged. Certainly, in their meeting of November, 1968, they were not able to find a way of solving the problem between Cardinal O'Boyle and his priests nor of serving as reconciling priestly mediators in the disagreement between the Archbishop of San Antonio and many of his priests and people. In situations such as this, the bishops stated they had no right to interfere in the affairs of another bishop. This decision reflects, perhaps, an unwillingness to face up to the implications of the Second Vatican Council, which explicitly states that a bishop has responsibilities, not only for his own diocese, but for the entire Church.

It has been often pointed out that United States Senators frequently seem to look upon the Senate as a club; consequently, they are very careful not to embarrass another club member by criticizing, or in any way "interfering with his affairs." There may well be a similar disposition on the part of a number of American bishops to look upon the national body of bishops as a club. Indeed, a well-known priest-sociologist told me of a conversation he had recently with a highly progressive archbishop who is one of the leaders in that assembly. When the priest asked why a number of bishops were so slow in really accepting and genuinely implementing many of the reforms called for by the Vatican Council, the archbishop replied: "You must understand that the bishops, as a rule, are reluctant to step on another bishop's toes. To many of them it is like belonging to a club and strict rules govern what one says or does." To which the priest-sociologist replied, "Then you had better tell the members that the clubhouse is on fire."

At the end of their meeting in November, the American bishops issued, in the name of all, a ten-thousand word document which touched on a number of points, particularly that of birth control. We shall return to their remarks on this subject in the next chapter. I simply wish to point out here that their remarks on this subject seemed to many to be rather ambiguous and consequently to lack the note of moral leadership which was expected. In answer to the question of just what the bishops had, in effect, intended to do at their meeting, a Catholic layman wrote the following in *The Commonweal,* a weekly journal owned and edited by Catholic laymen:

"What did they intend? . . . This observer is convinced that they proposed to do precisely what they in fact succeeded in doing: they intended simply to get away from the Washington-Hilton and out of town without being pinned down. By saying as much as possible as confusingly as possible, they succeeded in their intent. No one should be surprised about their goal. Getting out of town has been the name of the game for over 20 years when it comes to the annual statement of the American bishops."

I have personally known, over many years, the man who wrote this seemingly harsh judgment. He is not a young radical, concerned with overthrowing everything in the Church which does not please him; nor is he anticlerical in his outlook. For more than ten years, his work for a national association of Catholic laymen brought him into contact with many bishops throughout the United States. I know further that for him the Roman Catholic Church was a source and center of love, of loyalty, and of service as great as was his devotion to his family. I cannot, therefore, lightly dismiss his observations, and I feel it would be dishonest not to record them here.

Certainly, one major cause of the crisis of authority in the Church at the moment is that so many people who hold authority have, for whatever reason, failed to listen to the Second Vatican Council. They are like the little boy told by the zoo keeper that camels really do not store water in their humps. They can only say, "That ain't the way I learned it." Those of us unfortunately past the age of thirty hadn't learned about authority, freedom, and openness in the Church until the Council spoke to us; it is for that reason that the Council was, or should be, of such monumental importance in our lives as Christians.

And unless we—bishops as well as priests and laity—set about learning and living what the Council has taught, then the crisis of authority within the Church will grow even more damaging, and the "silent schism" may become articulate and divisive.

6

Headquarters:
That Infallible Pope

It is with great regret, now that we have reached the third floor, that I still cannot offer you a locale that is serene and peaceful, with the only sounds being the movement of people going efficiently about tasks which they understood. Once again, however, I must apologize because the scene, even here, is one of unusual bustle and subdued excitement. Members of the Italian nobility, who once held hereditary honorary titles within the Pope's staff, have been dismissed by Pope Paul. They are gathering up their fancy uniforms, stuffing them into trunks, and moving out, some with a dark scowl back and others deliberately bumping their trunks along the floor to express their displeasure.

The Pope has also attempted to modernize the Curia, the rough equivalent of a President's cabinet. These constitute a Pope's closest advisors, and have long held a position of authority and power within the Church since the Popes have relied so heavily upon them for advice and, when needed, support. Pope Paul has also internationalized the Curia, and we see a number of Italian bishops and cardinals packing their trunks and leaving as some American and European prelates arrive to take their places.

Most of the flurry, however, is caused by the press correspondents from all over the world. These have found, over the last five years, a great deal of reader interest in what happens in the Church. Consequently, they swarm outside Headquarters in much the same way that the press corps has long since set up its tents in the White House. Great changes are sweeping through the Church, amid great tensions. A rather recent press dispatch serves to make this fact clear in a rather dramatic way. As these lines are being written, a motion picture dealing with the Church of the future, *The Shoes of the Fisherman,* has just been released. Several months prior to its release, the following news story appeared from Rome, where much of the movie was filmed.

From "The Bells of St. Mary's" to "The Cardinal," the Catholic Church has always fascinated movie-makers, and the church has frequently cooperated. But the people making "The Shoes of the Fisherman" are learning that there have been some changes made; the church no longer sits still for the camera.

Metro-Goldwyn-Mayer and producer George Englund once thought it would be a great idea to film Morris West's 1963 best-selling novel about a Russian priest who becomes pope and proceeds to bring about a major updating of the church.

But since production started on "Shoes of the Fisherman," the film has been hit with one delay after another—while it catches up with the latest change announced by the Vatican or nervously awaits the next change.

"So much has happened in the Catholic Church since the book was published five years ago," said producer Englund, "that a good portion of the futuristic vision the author originally created suddenly reads like yesterday's news. It became a long and incessant job not only to keep up with Vatican activities but to retain the projection of events to come in our script."

The film . . . deals with such subjects as papal infallibility divorce, celibacy, and birth control but will offer no "solutions" for current controversies, Englund said.

Pope Paul must surely have been grateful that the movie did not attempt to "present solutions" to problems presently accounting for so much turmoil in the Church; indeed, he must often feel that he is getting far too many solutions already from within the Church, particularly on the vexed and related questions of

Papal infallibility and birth control. It is with these that we shall now attempt to deal.

On July 29, 1968, after years spent in coming to a decision, Pope Paul VI issued an encyclical, *Humane Vitae,* which upheld the Church's traditional opposition to every method of artificial birth control. Some observers have said that the date of this encyclical may turn out to be as historically significant as the date when Martin Luther posted his theses on the church door at Wittenburg, or the date when the Emperor Constantine gave the Christian Church in the fourth century its full freedom to exist within the Roman Empire.

Whatever the future verdict of history might be, it seems clear that the issuance of this encyclical, and its impact upon the Church, is for the contemporary Roman Catholic one of the major events of his lifetime. For, in all likelihood to Pope Paul's great surprise, his encyclical was not only not received with enthusiasm in many quarters of the Church, but many bishops, theologians, and lay people expressed publicly their inability fully to accept the Church's teaching. Nor did these hundreds of thousands feel that their inability to accept the encyclical mean that they should therefore, in all honesty, leave the Catholic Church. Indeed, many of them have explicitly stated that by opposing this encyclical, and the rather magisterial way in which it was promulgated, they are fighting to preserve the real tradition of the Church and are even supporting, rather than destroying, the proper understanding of the role of the Papacy.

When the encyclical was promulgated, it was officially announced by the Vatican that the document did not represent infallible teaching; its doctrine condemning artificial contraception could therefore, eventually be changed. Yet, despite this disclaimer, the encyclical has raised the whole issue of the Pope's infallibility to a greater pitch of discussion and controversy than at any time since the doctrine of Papal infallibility was pronounced in 1870 at the First Vatican Council. Obviously, we have an extremely snarled "net of the fisherman" on our hands and can hope to disentangle only a part of it in these pages.

The first thread that we must try to unsnarl is that of Papal infallibility. We have already explained in chapter 2 that the infallibility of the Pope does not mean that the Pope cannot be guilty of sin. This would be the divine gift of sinlessness, and while the Scriptures suggest that there may have been several human beings who possessed this gift, the Church has never claimed it for any Pope, beginning with the first who had thrice denied that he even knew "the Galilean," because he could not stand up under the taunts of a serving girl. Infallibility, then, has nothing to do with being supernaturally safeguarded from committing sin; it does mean that one who holds the highest office as teacher in the Christian Church is supernaturally protected from *teaching* falsehood, whether through his personal ignorance or even malice. It is necessary to point out at once that this preservation from the possibility of teaching falsehood is invested, not in a single human being, but in the community of Christians over whom this individual presides as head in the place of Christ. It is, then, the Church which is infallible, incapable of teaching or believing error when it is a question of what God has chosen to reveal to man, and who has entrusted that revelation to the Church.

The Pope, then, does not "discover" religious truths; he is not a theological Thomas Edison who bursts from his laboratory with a brilliant new idea. Indeed, the incapability of teaching theological falsehood rests precisely on the Church's belief that the Pope will proclaim only truths which have been part of the Christian belief from the beginning, but which might have been overlaid by the dust of centuries. The situation does not represent a unique one in human experience, and is very clear to an American. The Pope, in the Church, plays a role comparable to that of the Supreme Court. The Court does not write new legislation; that is not its function. The Court (despite the judgment of many about the Warren Court) does not rewrite the Constitution. Its only function is authoritatively to determine what is contained in the Constitution and in the legislation which has grown from it.

In similar fashion, the Pope can present for the belief of Catholics only a statement of what Catholics have always believed.

This is what is meant by saying that the Pope is infallible, protected from teaching falsehood, only when he speaks *ex cathedra,* only when he speaks from the Chair of Peter. In such cases, he interprets—for the whole Catholic Church—the traditional faith of that Church. The Chief Justice of the United States, in addressing a Kiwanis Club or the Ladies Bible Society, can say anything he wishes about various provisions or points of law in the Constitution. The value of what he says will be determined by the validity of what he says; if he is a wise man, his statements will probably have the ring of wisdom, but they will not constitute an authoritative, binding interpretation of the fundamental laws of the United States. Similarly, when the Pope speaks, no matter how solemnly, but not *ex cathedra,* what he says may also have the ring of wisdom, but will not constitute a fully authoriative interpretation of divine revelation.

Since the official proclamation, at the First Vatican Council in 1870, of Papal infallibility thus understood, a Pope has spoken *ex cathedra* only once—when, in 1950, Pope Pius XII proclaimed, as an article of Catholic belief, the Assumption of Mary into heaven. This meant that Roman Catholics were to believe that after her death, Mary's body was rejoined to her soul and that she has from that moment been in heaven as she was on earth. She knew death, but did not know the dissolution of her body after death.

This *ex cathedra* proclamation of Mary's Assumption has, since 1950, been a scandal to many, if not most, Protestants who look upon it as a classic example of what Popes are likely to do if they drink that heady wine of infallibility. We are not primarily concerned here with the meaning of Mary's Assumption, but are concerned with what its definitive declaration might show us about the nature and operation of Papal infallibility. It is noteworthy, first of all, that Pope Pius XII did not speak as though he had come across this interesting theological oddity in his reading and meditation and, because he was Pope, had decided that all other Catholics must share his belief. Rather, he points out evidences that from the infant Church to the twentieth century, Christians had maintained a belief in the Assumption. He also pointed out that he had ascertained, through inquiries to bishops and others, that this belief was still vigorously held in the Eastern Orthodox Churches and in some Protestant Churches as well as in the Roman Catholic Church. In a time of the world's history when the human body was once more being treated on a mass scale as lacking dignity or intrinsic worth; when despite the growing equality between the sexes, there was a disposition to treat women as objects, as things, the Pope felt it opportune to remind Christians of an ancient belief which extolled both the human body and womanhood.

From what has been said, it will be clear, I trust, that Papal infallibility is a gift given, not to an individual man who is the Pope, but to the Church, the Community of Faith, in which he holds the responsibility of teaching what that community believes, in articulating the faith which has come to it from the Apostles.

There has developed within the Catholic Church since the proclamation of infallibility in 1870, however, a most regrettable tendency. One might best describe it as "creeping infallibility." It represents a disposition to stretch the limits of infallibility far beyond the intention of the First Vatican Council, and begins to attach the same weight and significance to statements made by a Pope even in addressing a crowd of pilgrims from his balcony overlooking St. Peter's Square as would be attached to a solemn statement of belief proclaimed *ex cathedra*. "Creeping infallibility" is equivalent to considering as an authoritative interpretation of the Constitution what the Chief Justice might say in addressing a convention of Masons, or a meeting of the National Council of Churches. The Church has had an epidemic of "creeping infallibility" and we are only now beginning to realize the harm it has inflicted.

The vexed question of birth control shows clearly how "creeping infallibility" works. It treats papal statements on this subject as fully binding and authoritative—*ex cathedra*—even when these statements were not issued *ex cathedra.* To understand this better, we shall have to take a brief look at the history of the Christian Church's attitude toward contraception. The problem seems not to have arisen in the first three centuries of the Church's existence. It is not that contraceptive methods and devices were unknown at this period, since contraception was widely practiced in the Roman Empire. The Church, however, made no pronouncements concerning it. From the fourth century onward, we find strong condemnations of contraception voiced by St. Augustine and other theologians; but it must also be remembered that the Church, within this period and for centuries later, did not have a fully developed theology of marriage. The primary purpose of marriage was seen to be the procreation of children, and whatever directly interfered with that purpose was considered gravely sinful.

When the situation seemed to call for it, the Church repeated these condemnations of contraception. It was not, however, until the second half of the nineteenth century, when contraceptive devices became more reliable, inexpensive and readily obtainable, that the Church began to repeat, with such insistence, its conviction that contraception was against the law of man's nature and hence an offense against man's Creator.

The most formal statement of this position came in 1930, with the promulgation of an encyclical by Pope Pius XI on Marriage, *Casti Connubii.* In this encyclical, Pope Pius wrote movingly and beautifully of the human values in marriage, and reflected the growing awareness, in all the Christian Churches, of the immense value of interpersonal union in marital love and of the central role of the family in human society. He also repeated, however, the traditional view that the primary purpose of marriage was "the procreation and education of children." Consequently, any direct interference with the procreative nature of the marital act was to be considered seriously sinful. This encyclical, it will be noted, was a letter addressed to the entire Roman Catholic world, but it did not present its teachings as infallible.

Pope Pius XII, several times in his papacy, repeated the teachings of *Casti Connubii,* and it should be noted here that he repeated them in addressing, not the entire Church, but specific meetings of Catholics in the medical profession. One such address was given to a meeting of Italian midwives, another to a meeting of Italian physicians. We are certainly far removed from the circumstances of an *ex cathedra* proclamation of Church teaching when we are gathered with Italian midwives or physicians in a hall in the Vatican.

Nevertheless, because of "creeping infallibility," there was a tendency on the part of most Roman Catholics, including bishops and theologians, to treat these statements as if they were fully binding and as if, indeed, the entire discussion of contraception, by whatever means, were completely closed.

Several things happened, however, between the death of Pius XII and the convening of the Second Vatican Council. The anovulent pill had been refined and represented a more reliable, inexpensive, and "aesthetic" means of birth prevention. There had been within Catholicism a deepening realization of mutual love between husband and wife as an end of marriage at least as important as that of the procreation of children, and there had been a fuller exploration of responsible parenthood. Neither the "holiness" of a marriage nor its healthiness was to be judged primarily by the number of children it had produced. Indeed, this last factor, the number of children, itself came under close scrutiny because the Roman Catholic world began at last to recognize what the rest of the world had known for some time: there was a population explosion and a population problem which could affect the quality of human life on this planet in both the present and the future.

These new factors were very much on the minds of the bishops and their theological advisors when they assembled for the Second Vatican Council. In the third session of that Council the commission entrusted with drawing up the documents on *The Church in the Modern World* proposed to deal with marriage and to raise, at least, the issue of contraception. The statements of this commission on marriage were presented to the bishops and approved; they represent an extension and development of earlier Church teachings on the sacredness and beauty of marriage, and enforce the idea of responsible parenthood.

The question of contraception, however, was removed from discussion by Pope Paul, who indicated that he wished to reserve this matter to himself. There may well have been very good reasons for his having done so; the fact that the Church might change its position on this extremely delicate matter which affected so profoundly the lives of millions could not, perhaps, be satisfactorily resolved in discussion and debate involving more than two thousand bishops with much work to do and little time in which to do it.

Pope Paul then appointed a commission, not only of bishops and theologians, but of laymen and women including psychologists, physicians and demographers to assist him in formulating what would be the Church's teaching on this point. This advisory commission met over a period of several years; it eventually produced two reports, a majority one and a minority one. It is significant that the majority opinion advocated a change in Church teaching and recognized the morality of contraception when a married couple had legitimate reasons for not wishing further children. The International Congress of Lay People was brought into being after the Council to inform Church authorities of the opinions and attitudes of lay people throughout the world. Meeting in 1967, this Congress expressed itself, by an overwhelming majority, to be in favor of changing the Church's traditional view on contraception. Each couple should determine the number of children they would wish to have, consonant with the principle of generous but responsible parenthood.

On July 29, 1968, Pope Paul issued his long awaited statement on the subject in the encyclical *Humane Vitae*. In it, he reaffirmed, in strong terms, the Church's traditional opposition to any form of birth limitation apart from the so-called rhythm method. In upholding the traditional view, he employed the traditional arguments, even while also expressing, in sincere and effective language, the Church's view of the sanctity of marriage, the beauty of marital love, and the irreplaceable role of the family in human society.

Many millions of Catholics welcomed the reassertion of this prohibition against birth limitation. Perhaps surprising to the Pope and his advisors, however, was the fact that millions also expressed their disappointment and dismay that he had done so. For many such Catholics, the question had become one to be solved by their consciences as individuals, since they knew best their own circumstances as married couples and actual or potential parents.

The question for these had become once again the question of the relation between authority and freedom. In their view, it is practically, if not theologically, impossible for a document such as *Humane Vitae* to lay down a norm of behavior applicable, without modifications, for married people all over the world, regardless of their social and economic environment and their personal development.

It is interesting and important to note that the claims of both freedom and authority were supported by the official response of many national hierarchies to *Humane Vitae*. With varying degrees of emphasis, the bishops of Holland, Belgium, France, and Germany pointed out that the Papal encyclical should be received with reverence, and studied with care. The Papal teaching should be used to assist married couples in forming their conscience on the question of family limitation. These bishops also, however, pointed out that the conscience of the individual is inviolable, and in those situations where a married couple felt that they could not abide by the teaching of the encyclical, they could follow their conscience without moral guilt.

Other national groups of bishops, notably in England and many Latin-American countries, called for obedience to the encyclical, insisting that it was the authoritative and principal determinant of what a Catholic couple's conscience should be. The reactions were not, of course, confined to bishops. In the United States, a group of theologians at the Catholic University of America drew up a statement insisting, contrary to *Humane Vitae,* that couples had the *right* to practice contraception if their consciences dictated. It will be noticed that this statement is stronger than the statements of those national hierarchies which suggested that Catholics could follow their conscience if they could not follow the Pope. This statement, originating with a group of theologians at Catholic University, has now drawn the signature of six-hundred priests and theologians throughout the United States at the date of this writing.

Groups of lay people in dioceses throughout the United States have also registered their disapproval of the Pope's position, and in Germany five thousand laymen at their annual Catholic Day in the autumn of 1968, adopted a resolution which advised the Pope that they could not accept his encyclical's teaching. To these collective voices have been added those of many of the Church's most prominent theologians, speaking individually, who have pointed out that the encyclical is not infallible. If, therefore, it is not *certainly true,* it may, by that same token, be wrong. It is hard to discount as exaggerated the statement of one such eminent theologian, Hans Küng, when he says, "I fear the encylical creates a second Galileo case."

Again, it would be misleading to suggest that all of the response to the encyclical on the part of theologians and lay people has been negative. A number of highly competent theologians have declared their support, as theologians, of the encyclical; a national group of lay people has been formed with the express purpose of declaring, to the American Church, their unswerving loyalty and obedience to the Pope on this precise issue.

It was against this background of storm clouds and lightning that the American bishops met in November, 1968, to frame their pastoral letter in such a way that they might, if possible, bring a measure of peace and tranquility to the Church, cast into such upheaval by *Humanae Vitae.*

We have earlier described the turbulent scene which met the bishops when they convened, and one can only sympathize with their efforts to think, discuss, and compose above the sounds of folk-singing and protest coming from below. There was, of course, division of opinion among the bishops themselves, and it was necessary first to draft a document which would win the approval of more than two hundred bishops even before, hopefully, it might win the acceptance of a majority of American Catholics.

When the bishops had completed their pastoral letter, after drafting sessions which often went until four A.M., the document urged faithfulness to the Pope's teaching in *Humanae Vitae,* but urged those couples who could not follow it not to abandon their sacramental lives as Catholics. The bishops affirmed the objective evil of contraception itself, but did recognize that individuals might not be able themselves to recognize it as evil, or live up to the demands of not practicing contraception even if they did recognize it as an objective evil.

The pastoral letter of the United States bishops gives very strong, unambiguous statements on issues such as foreign aid, the right of an individual to selective conscientious objection, the questionable morality of nuclear deterrents. On the question of birth control, however, it would seem to embody ambiguities. These lines are being written shortly after the letter itself has been issued, and in the Catholic journals before me I read of some of the most prominent bishops in the United States denying that their pastoral letter was in any way a "compromise" or "relaxation" of the Pope's encyclical on contraception. On the same page of these journals, I also read statements from the dissident priests in Washington to the effect that the pastoral letter of the bishops is "clear vindication" of the position of these priests on the right of the individual to make his own decision regarding birth control in the light of his own conscience.

All of this, I fully realize, may seem somewhat confusing to the Protestant reader. I can only assure him, in such a case, that he has begun to feel something of what it is like to be an American

Catholic at this moment. It is not necessarily a bad feeling, or one that gives rise to panic. It is rather more one of surprise and consequent challenge—like diving into a lake in the spring, only to realize that the winds and waves have shifted the bottom since last summer. One can no longer stand where he stood before, but is not thereby prevented from swimming.

One last consideration must be entered here. We have spoken earlier of the fact that the Second Vatican Council envisioned new ways for authority to operate within the Church. Among these new ways was a continuing consultation, not only with bishops throughout the Church, but, to the degree possible, ascertaining the opinions of the majority of the Church itself throughout the world, most notably its lay people. We have already seen that, in coming to his decision on contraception, Pope Paul chose not to accept the majority report of the Advisory Commission which he himself had created.

He did not, further, seemingly give much importance to the resolution of the International Congress of the Laity meeting in Rome in the autumn of 1967. The meeting of the laity coincided with the first International Congress of bishops who were, following the principle of collegiality of the Second Vatican Council, regularly to assist the Pope through their deliberations and advise in the administration of the Church. These bishops were, for the most part, elected by their fellow bishops in a given country to represent them in the task of serving as advisors to the Pope. Many people, including many bishops, had expected that the Pope would consult with this handpicked, highly representative group of bishops on the question of birth control. The question was, however, not even on the agenda.

Before Pope Pius XII defined the doctrine of the Assumption of Mary, he took a sounding of the belief of Catholics throughout the world. Pope Paul seemingly took no such sounding; if he had, he would have learned that a number of surveys made in the United States alone agreed that more than 50 percent of its priests and 70 percent of its lay people felt that contraception was in itself morally acceptable, and that the decision to practice it was primarily the responsibility of a married couple.

Up to this point, we have been dealing with infallibility and, specifically, the relation of infallibility to *Humanae Vitae,* as though these were questions of interest and concern exclusively to Catholics. We have all learned, however, that the world is round and there is no longer any corner wherein a major Christian Church can act as if its affairs were no one else's business—particularly when Pope Paul supported the view against contraception by resorting to the morality of natural law—a morality which on important matters is supposedly as obvious to any man of intelligence as it is to a Catholic.

The reactions to *Humanae Vitae* of the world outside Roman Catholicism were sharply and clearly expressed by a member of the Communications Department of the World Council of Churches. Dr. Albert van den Heuvel knows both the United States and Europe, and has spent considerable time in the emerging nations as well. I must also point out that in conducting television interviews with him at the World Council in Geneva, I found him quite critical of certain aspects of the World Council itself. My own estimate of Dr. van den Heuvel is that, like Nathaniel, he is "an Israelite without guile"—a type which can frequently be uncomfortable even as they are always necessary.

An Associated Press dispatch from Rome, some six weeks after the appearance of *Humanae Vitae,* reported on a press conference given by Dr. van den Heuvel:

A World Council of Churches official said today Pope Paul VI's birth control encyclical ignored every major theme of the Vatican Ecumenical Council and offended Protestants and others who were using contraceptives.

The Rev. Dr. Albert van den Heuvel, director of the council's communications department, told a news conference that Orthodox Christian Church reaction to the document was highly favorable and that a small number of Protestants and Anglicans also sided with Pope Paul.

"But the majority of Protestant and Anglican Church leaders and theologians were either puzzled, disappointed or very contrary," van den Heuvel said.

"The big words of the Vatican Council," van den Heuvel states, "were *dialogue, collegiality, ecumenical movement, pastoral approach, openness* to the *rest of the world.*

"Not any of these five major points played a role in the teaching of *Humanae Vitae.*"

Confused and diverse reactions of national communities of Roman Catholic bishops are evidence that there had been little or no dialogue between the Vatican and the rest of the Church on birth control teaching, van den Heuvel said. He added that this also went against collegiality, the principle by which cardinals and bishops help the Pope govern the Church.

Neither, he said, were any Protestant theologians or church leaders consulted. He said this was a slight to ecumenism.

"And the Pope has spoken more about the sustenance of papal authority than about a pastoral concern for the flock," the official declared. "The people of God have felt this. Surveys show they have changed their habits on the use of contraceptives hardly at all."

Turning to the offensiveness [which] he said the encyclical held for many Protestants, van den Heuvel said: "The treatment of those who use contraceptives as potential libertines was hardly taken as a friendly word.

"The Pope's remarks on morality are offensive to those who have made a conscience decision to use artificial birth control devices."

The choice of a Protestant spokesman on these points is deliberate, simply to show how deeply, in this ecumenical era, decisions and statements of the Pope affect other Churches. Professor van den Heuvel's judgments are, in essence, no different from statements made by such distinguished Roman Catholic theologians as Karl Rahner, George Tavard, Gregory Baum, Charles Curran, and many others.

Most of the rather heated discussion following *Humanae Vitae* has centered around its anticontraception position. The more important point is rarely recognized: even if the encyclical had supported the conscience of the individual to practice birth control in certain circumstances, the fact that Pope Paul would have announced this decision "single-handedly" would also have made his way of acting antiecumenical, anticollegial, and antidialogue. It would, as a consequence, have been very serious in its impact both within and without the Roman Catholic Church, since it would represent the way in which a Pope was no longer expected to act after the Second Vatican Council.

7

Priests and Nuns:
Revolt of the Robots?

We have gone through so much confusion and noise, you and I, that I deeply wish for your sake that we could come to some portion of the house where quiet reigns and peace prevails. I am afraid, however, that we will find the din increasing as we move toward the servants quarters, and consider the present situation of priests and nuns within American Catholicism.

It will be clear, of course, that the term "servants quarters" is an honorable one, since the very term "minister" as used among Protestants means servant. Part of the problem of Catholic priests and nuns today lies precisely in the fact that they wish to *serve* the Church and their fellowman in ways which their bishops frequently do not approve and often do not understand. We will go first to the priest's quarters, and I would ask you to show surprise at nothing you might hear or see.

There was a time, not long ago, when such a request would have been unnecessary. Priests worked hard, for the most part, at their appointed tasks and their appointed tasks all dealt, directly or indirectly, with the care and feeding of their spiritual flock. They were pastors of parishes, or assistants to pastors. They were hospital chaplains, prison chaplains, military chaplains and many of the forty thousand priests in the United States taught something to somebody in a Catholic high school, college, or seminary. Occasionally, of course, a priest would encounter severe personal problems in his efforts to live up to the high demands of his calling; a comparative few would abandon their priesthood and marry. In such a case, they would usually go to some city where they were not known and begin a completely different way of life in completely different surroundings. Others would fall victim to alcoholism, but in a smaller ratio than that of doctors or lawyers. Inevitably, too, some would suffer severe nervous breakdowns, although, again, in no greater proportion than that observed among members of other intensely demanding professions.

For the most part, however, the Catholic priest went about his duties with a sense of dedication and even cheerfulness. The demands made, particularly upon a pastor, were rather heavy and perhaps inordinately tied to the awful and awesome business of raising sufficient funds to keep afloat the parish "plant"— church, parochial school, rectory, and a residence for the nuns teaching in the school. All this, of course, was before Pope John XXIII decided to open that window. Once opened, the wind blew through with such force that the window could not really be slammed shut again, despite the efforts of many within the Church to do so.

Certainly, the gales have blown through priests' rectories and have shaken more than the draperies. There is, as a result, a profound change sweeping at the moment through the priesthood, not only in the United States, but in Northern Europe, some portions of Latin America and even Ireland. Wherever the words of the Second Vatican Council have been taken seriously, and new hopes and expectations aroused by its new vision of *the people of God on pilgrimage* through the rest of the twentieth century, there one finds ferment. It is particularly the younger priests who have experienced the keenest disappointment when their superior or bishop seemed to flag down their enthusiasm. Where that enthusiasm could not be flagged down, it was often shot down and the result has been a dramatic, if not traumatic, tension within the priesthood.

Reliable estimates indicate that in the year 1968 more than 475 American priests have left the priesthood. A priest friend of mine in Texas, ordained twelve years, told me recently that of the thirty-eight men ordained with him at the North American College in Rome, nineteen have either left the priesthood or have been suspended in the exercise of their priestly office. I would think it safe to say that almost every American Catholic lay person knows, with some degree of intimacy, at least one priest who has either abandoned the priesthood or fallen into the displeasure of his religious superiors within the past five years.

Not all of these priests who have departed, obviously, represent a real and tragic loss to the Church; some should never have been admitted to the priesthood in the first place. Their departure, which in a few cases represents a gain to the publishers of their rather sensational "exposes," does not really represent a loss to the Church. In the case of most of these men, however, the fact that they could no longer remain within the priesthood represents a drain upon one of the strongest resources which the Church possesses in the person of her priests.

I have had a privilege denied to the great majority of Catholic laymen—the opportunity to come to know many priests of all ages in almost every part of the United States. I have spent many hours talking with them in bull sessions in hotel rooms during conventions, when the speeches and workshops were over and the most meaningful discussions could begin. To render my credentials a bit more respectable, I must also add that I have lectured often at seminaries and colleges and, even despite the lecture, later been offered the hospitality of the faculty recreation room.

Very often I would be the only lay person in these gatherings, but the priests were good enough to extend their trust and Christian love to me, and would talk either as though I were not there, or were one of them. I have come to see the Church—both pre- and post-conciliar—through their eyes as well as my own. I have also, through them, gotten some feeling of the very texture of the priesthood—the rough, uncoated fibres and the smooth, splendidly beautiful threads.

To a greater degree, perhaps, than most laymen, I can number priests among my closest, most cherished friends. They have shared our home often, have exchanged confidences, hopes and fears with my wife and me, and have broken with us the bread of friendship, shared the rich wine of fraternal love.

It is, then, the memory of many moments, the sight of many faces that are before me as I write. Whatever value these lines may have is that I am simply sharing with the Protestant reader what Catholic priests have given me, often unaware of the value of the gift, or even that it was being given.

The men I have met are, in greatest measure, authentic human beings, endowed, not with heroic sanctity, but with that holiness which is less charismatic but perhaps more remarkable: the courage to rise each morning, blow into flame the coals of faith, hope, and love, and move out into the new day—a day which demands of the priest, far more than it does of the lay person, that he be, like his High Priest, "the man for others"—all others.

I have noticed another quality in most of the priests I have met: an honesty about themselves. Extending the classical definition a bit, we might describe man as an unfeathered biped who cooks his food, and has an almost infinite capacity for self-deception. Whether by grace or training, priests seem to have somewhat less of that last quality than most nonpriests of my acquaintance, including myself.

I have never encountered such candor, such ruthless honesty with others about oneself, as I have noted again and again in groups of priests locked in dialogue.

Perhaps I have met only the best, but neither the law of probabilities nor the usual workings of divine Providence would tend to support that hypothesis. I think I have seen this quality of honesty-to-self in priests because unmistakably, like an elephant on the piano, it is really there.

Good men, honest men. And yet the crisis in the priesthood is growing to frightening proportions. No one has the right to use a "man-the-lifeboat" phrase such as that without serious warrant.

I think the warrant is serious. The loss of religious women to the Church is grave, and bespeaks the fact that thousands of nuns are ardently hoping for a reform of their lives that goes beyond hemlines and the daily schedule. The laity, in increasing numbers, are making waves, and it will serve to wash the scuppers if the bark of Peter ships some water as a result of their efforts.

But neither the laity nor the nun plays quite the hinge role in the Church that the priest does. A crisis in the priesthood signals a crisis in the Church precisely because the ordained priest is functionally inseparable from the Church and the Church is functionally inoperative without the priesthood.

One of the reasons for the crisis of the priesthood is the authoritarian style of exercising authority shown by a number of bishops in the United States. What is striking is that, in almost every such case, the priests in difficulty are among the finest priests in the bishop's jurisdiction. I know personally no less than ten priests, in as many dioceses, who are either currently under suspension or who have, after such suspension, asked for laicization. Not one of these is a problem priest; neither Punch nor Judy has accounted for their incurring the displeasure of their bishop. They are, in the judgment of those who know them best, splendid priests. Their major mistake has been to take the letter and the spirit of Vatican II more seriously than has their bishop.

In disciplining such priests, their bishops have cited the virtue of prudence and "the scandal of the flock"; they cannot cite, however, any document of the Council which these priests have violated. Indolent priests, weak priests, worldly priests in these same dioceses are not touched by episcopal censure; that seems reserved for those priests who have attempted to implement Vatican II under the jurisdiction of a bishop who seems to prefer the cool shadow of the pyramid labeled Vatican I.

One of the principal causes, then, for the present crisis in the Roman Catholic priesthood lies in the fact that so many feel that they are being treated by their superiors as things rather than as people, as objects to be used for a function, rather than as people who can function. In a survey of eighteen thousand American priests—almost one third of their total number—a priest-sociologist, Joseph Fichter, found that a principal complaint of the average priest is that he was dealt with like a tab on an organization chart.

There was also a strong feeling recorded by the priests that they had no effective "court of appeal" in those cases where their view clashed with that of their bishop. He held all the best cards, and when he slammed them on the table, the game was over. This was one of the principal complaints of the priests in Washington who had been disciplined by Cardinal O'Boyle, just as it was the situation which led a number of priests in San Antonio to request the retirement of their archbishop.

There are, fortunately, some hopeful signs; if there were not, the only decent thing to do would be to close this chapter now and head for the cyclone shelter. In many dioceses, including the largest, associations of priests have been formed. Their purpose is not to serve as a labor union for priests, pressing for better working conditions. Their purpose rather is to assist the bishop to be a better, that is, a more pastoral, bishop and assist the priests to be more effective in their priestly ministry. In a number of these dioceses, personnel committees have been formed either to approve a priest's change of assignment if suggested by the bishop, or to themselves determine changes of assignment and submit their recommendations to the bishop. In either case, the bishop is spared feeling like the centurion in the Gospel who says, "to this one go and he goeth; to this one, come and he cometh." These priests' associations have, in most cases, also set up mediation boards to act in those cases where a bishop seems to have a grievance against one of his priests or vice versa.

In addition to these local associations of priests, a National Association of Priests has been formed; its credentials are beyond suspicion, its leadership is intelligent, its membership enthusiastic and devoted.

I have called developments such as these hopeful signs, but it must be remembered that they are merely that. If associations such as this grow not only in number but in effectiveness, if there is genuine dialogue carried on between each bishop and his priests, who are in the words of the Second Vatican Council the bishops' "friends and brothers," then the present crisis of the priesthood will prove to have been gain, not loss. A more committed priesthood, perhaps fewer in number, will more than make up for those priests who have been tragically lost to the Catholic community over the past several years.

Another reason for the decline of vocations to the priesthood, and even more seriously, for the exodus from the priesthood is the factor of celibacy—the provision in the major part of the Roman Catholic Church that a priest may not marry. It is important to notice at the outset that the requirement of celibacy for ordination to the priesthood is purely a matter of the Church's own laws, and has no real roots in Scripture or the tradition of the Church through early centuries. The fact that Roman Catholics were not permitted to eat meat on Friday was also a result of the Church's law, and had no roots in Divine revelation. As a consequence, the Church could abrogate the law of abstinence from meat on Friday whenever it seemed that the law no longer served its original purpose of requiring Catholics regularly to practice this penance or was, indeed, working a hardship on certain Catholics. Such seemed to be the case several years ago, and the law of Friday abstinence was abolished.

The Church could do the same with the law or priestly celibacy whenever it seemed to the Church that the law was no longer helpful, or that it worked a hardship upon certain sections of the Church. This situation seems not to have developed, at least according to the Pope's understanding of the case, and consequently he has reaffirmed the law of celibacy in an encyclical issued in 1967. There are many, within the Church, who feel that the Pope has not read accurately what is happening within the priesthood and who are therefore urging a revision of the law requiring all priests to be unmarried.

Among the original purposes of this law was the feeling of the Church, following St. Paul, that the married man must give his time, thought, and energies to his family as well as to his stewardship of other souls. To this scriptural observation were added practical considerations: the priest who had, as it were, only himself to support obviously need be paid less salary than would a priest who was also husband and father. Such a priest was also more mobile, and could be moved from one assignment to another at the expense of fewer and more shallow roots than could a priest with a settled, family-centered domicile.

The last of these two arguments, the practical ones, have been questioned in our time because of what is seen taking place outside the Church itself. Americans form the most mobile society known to history. The personnel of large corporations are picked up like a kitten by the scruff and are set down with their families wherever the needs of the corporation dictate. It has, indeed, been suggested that if one really wants to see the world he should join, not the Navy, but IBM, General Foods, or a large oil company.

Catholics have become aware also of a situation which bears more immediately on the supposed effectiveness of a celibate clergy. As ecumenism has shattered the walls which separated those of different faiths from one another, Catholics have come to realize that married ministers and married rabbis seem no less zealous, spiritual, or effective than do their own unmarried priests. My wife and I have often had the experience of coming to know such married clergy and their wives and have been struck, in almost every case, by the fact that the wife seemed to share so deeply her husband's sacred calling. Theirs was, in effect, a dual vocation.

Many other Catholics, including priests, have shared this same experience and for this reason have begun to question whether St. Paul's observation on the unmarried minister of the gospel is really applicable to all ministers of the gospel.

Further, as Catholic theologians began to develop, largely over the last decade, a theology of marriage at once more realistic and idealistic than the Church had ever known, many began to realize that the union of two in one flesh, achieved in a sacramental marriage, could represent for each a spiritual as well as personal fulfilment. In other words, some doctors began to suspect that the medicine they prescribe to others might really be pretty good after all.

So far as I can determine, there are no statistics which would strongly establish that the law of celibacy is the principal factor causing so many men to leave the priesthood. I have seen some surveys which indicate that it is a major factor, and others which make it comparatively minor. After leaving the priesthood, many men do marry; but it would be rash to conclude, on the basis of present evidence, that because they have married after leaving the priesthood they must have left the priesthood in order to marry.

 Regardless of what the situation may prove to have been, it seems increasingly clear that the Roman Catholic Church will be faced with a shortage of priests throughout the world. Practical considerations, then, may well force the Church in the not-too-distant future to abrogate the present law of priestly celibacy. In all likelihood, however, the abrogation of this law will not shake or call into question the positive value of *chosen* celibacy, for the history of the Church, present and past, indicates the great value, less to the individual than to the community, of those who have chosen to be "eunuchs for the sake of the kingdom." Christ, the Lord of the Church, will continue to summon a certain number to practice an all-inclusive love, with the greater measure of spiritual freedom which this entails. Responding to this specific call, there will always be those who choose to lead out their lives of priestly service in the closest imitation of the Great High Priest.

Before we visit the nun's section of the servants quarters, it may be well to check a few possible myths and misconceptions concerning them. Both of us recognize, I think, that there still remain among American Protestants some pockets of prejudice and absolutely malicious misunderstanding of nuns. *Maria Monk,* that pernicious best-seller of the last century, continues to have an influence among a certain type of Protestant who has had little opportunity to learn very much about either his own faith or Roman Catholicism. Convents have never been the equivalent of ecclesiastical brothels, and the mere suggestion, understandably, makes Catholics bridle. For we know nuns. We have been impressed by their complete dedication to the work of God, and have seen that their vowed virginity seemed to have been the source of so much of that gentleness and cheerful charity which we associate with most nuns we have known.

Certain changes have been taking place in convents, however, which we Catholics ourselves must become accustomed to—and not every Catholic is managing to do so gracefully. For Catholics past thirty-five, a nun was readily identified by her dress: yards and yards of serge which swathed her from neck to ankles, a veil which covered her head completely and very often left visible only her face. When their feet were visible under the long garb, it was seen that they wore black shoes of the kind affected by police-women. I often wondered where the nuns could buy their shoes, since the last for them had come obviously from another century.

Now all this is being changed, and the change in nuns' dress is a rather dramatic symbol of the changes taking place in their entire way of life. Until the recent past, most nuns, even during daytime, were to travel with a companion, usually another nun from the same community. This custom was, of course, a holdover from Europe in the seventeenth and eighteenth centuries, when no decent woman went out alone. Such was the temper of those times that a woman unaccompanied was either thought to be of rather loose morals or at least ran the risk of being accosted on the streets by predatory men. The nuns' dress was also a hangover from earlier centuries in Europe, where most of religious communities of women had been founded. At the time these communities were founded, most nuns wore the garb of their day, precisely in order that they would not be conspicuous by their dress, the material and design of which also identified them with the poorer classes.

Obviously, these features, well-suited to other countries and earlier times, became increasingly out of place in the modern world. I remember taking a graduate course in Anglo-Saxon in a class where there were two nun students. The course was a required one, and was conducted by a demanding and somewhat irascible German-born professor. I recall his snorting and muttering when he discovered that, although only two nuns were actually taking the course, there were four nuns in his class, since each nun was accompanied by a companion. One companion read assiduously for her own course in Comparative Literature, and the fact that she never once looked up at the professor nettled him somewhat. His patience would occasionally, however, explode into bits when, through his attempts to explain certain beauties of Anglo-Saxon grammar, there could also be heard the click of knitting needles coming from the second nun-companion, who completed an entire black sweater while her colleague was completing the course in Anglo-Saxon.

How quickly all this has changed! Two years ago I was attending the national convention of the Religious Education Association in Chicago. The Association has been, from its foundation in 1903, an interfaith organization of religious educators. Over the last ten years, Roman Catholics have joined the association in far greater numbers than ever before, and nuns attended the conventions in great numbers. It was less possible now, than at earlier conventions, to see at a glance just how many nuns made up the convention assembly, because the nuns in the meantime were changing from their traditional garb into suits and dresses similar to those worn by professional and businesswomen. I happened to be in an elevator with, among others, two nuns and the president of a Protestant seminary. After complimenting the nuns on the modernity and simple good taste of their new garb, he turned to another young lady, hatless, but wearing a trim gray suit. "And what community do you belong to, Sister?" he asked as the elevator stopped at the lobby. "United Airlines," she replied with a smile as she went through the elevator doors.

Current changes in nuns' dress, however, are far less important than the changes taking place within the entire structure of their lives. Most of the one hundred and eighty thousand nuns in the United States had either taught in the Catholic schools and colleges across the country, or served as administrators and nurses in Catholic hospitals. Their way of life was a disciplined one, with regular hours set aside for prayer, both private and communal. They were not, as a rule, permitted to be outside their convent in the evening without a very grave reason. Many of them were not permitted to eat anywhere with lay people, and some communities would not permit their members to visit their own homes, even in the case of a death within the family. It has now been generally recognized that no matter how justified such rules may have been at one time, they no longer serve the proper religious development of the nun.

If one had to sum up in a phrase what underlies the almost revolutionary changes taking place among nuns, he would say that these changes have taken place to further the growth of mature, responsible Christian women. The nuns, to a greater degree than any other sector of American Catholicism, have taken the Second Vatican Council with the utmost seriousness and are trying to incorporate its spirit within their lives. For this reason, considerable experimentation, not only in dress but in style of Christian living, is taking place among the nuns.

While continuing to teach, for example, some nuns now live in small communities of three or four, in a rented apartment close to their school. This has taken place particularly where the school is situated in a poor neighborhood, in an effort to have the sisters exhibit their care and concern for the total neighborhood by living among its people, not behind the security of convent walls. Nuns are now attending graduate courses at Harvard, Yale, Columbia, the University of Chicago, and dozens of other major universities. They live either in a nearby apartment or in a dormitory with other women students and are usually indistinguishable in dress from all but the most "mod" coed.

Some nuns also serve as caseworkers or administrative supervisors in state and municipal welfare operations, and several work in Federal bureaus connected with our present national efforts to curb and cure poverty. Nuns have also shown themselves, as a group, enthusiastic ecumenists and hundreds now work with those of other faiths in ecumenical slum projects as well as participating in high-level ecumenical discussions and formal courses of study. So marked has been the interest of nuns in ecumenism that the director of the summer program at a well-known Protestant seminary in the east told me, quite seriously, that he might in the future have to limit the number of nuns admitted. "They are," he commented with an admixture of gladness and sadness, "almost half of our student summer population, and I am afraid that will start keeping Protestants from their own seminary."

Recently, an entire community of American missionary nuns affiliated themselves with the Division of Overseas Ministries of the National Council of Churches, which represents the missionary boards and agencies of most of the major Protestant denominations in the United States. This new alliance does not mean, of course, that the nuns are weakening their affiliation with Roman Catholicism, or that they were trying to shore up their own inadequacies by joining a strong Protestant body. The nuns in question, the Medical Mission Sisters, operate thirty-three hospitals in fourteen countries of Asia, Africa, and Latin America and care for more than one million patients yearly. More than fifty members of the order are physicians, and the others are nurses, pharmacists, and medical technicians. This outreach of a Roman Catholic community of nuns toward sharing their missionary labors with other Christians is almost a symbol of the new spirit of the new nun.

The same openness toward the new, this same willingness to lay aside the old, is also shown in the efforts currently being made by most communities of nuns to rewrite their rules and constitutions. I have seen the new legislation of five different communities of nuns, and each of them is a model legislative document.

The emphasis is not upon the solidity and well-being of the community, but upon the full development of the individual within and through the community. The emphasis upon responsible freedom and free responsibility, the understanding of authority as service, and the place of the Holy Spirit in the direction of both the individual and the community embody the directives of the Second Vatican Council more fully, at least in my judgment, than do any other of the new groupings which have recently been formed, including priest associations, diocesan senates and national organizations of lay people.

The history of the Roman Catholic Church in America would have been considerably different without the communities of religious women. Whatever the future of the Roman Catholic Church in America may be, it seems safe to say that it will be written, in great part, by the devotion and service of thousands of intelligent and gracious women who form the communities of nuns.

It is unfortunate that, even in this time of increasing cordial contacts between Protestants and Catholics, many Protestants still have never had the opportunity to meet and converse with a nun. It will be increasingly difficult to strike up a conversation with one on the street, because one might find it hard to know now whether or not the lady is a nun. I would take the liberty of suggesting, however, that if any reader of this book felt a desire to know what nuns are all about, and what makes them tick, he might simply present himself at the door of a nearby convent and explain why he had come. He might not be surprised, but he would certainly be pleased at the resulting experience of meeting Christian women who seem blissfully unaware of their heroism and inner beauty.

8

The Laity:
Pray, Pay, and Obey?

The next stage in our visit calls for us to go "below decks," to
the basement which supports the entire edifice of the Roman
Catholic faith. Not only are there incomparably more lay persons
than there are bishops, priests, and nuns, but the bishops and
priests have no function to perform unless it is performed for the
spiritual welfare of the laity. This, of course, is the basic truth
about the role of the laity in every church. It seems, however, to
have been grossly overlooked in the centuries of Roman Catholicism after the Protestant Reformation.

What happened in those centuries could be summarized by
saying that ends became means, and means became ends—in
much the same way, for example, that in the Roman Republic
before its fall, or in France before the Revolution of 1798, those
in authority had come to the surprising conclusion that the
majority of their subjects had, for their major purpose, keeping in
authority those who were in authority. Their function, in short,
was to keep crowns in place upon royal heads, and support
royalty in the style to which it had become accustomed.

When informed that most of the French people lacked bread,
Queen Marie Antoinette is supposed to have said, "then let them
eat cake." The equivalent has often been said, not by the words
of certain bishops, but by their actions, in their implicit assumption that the Church really was the pyramid which we have
described in chapter 5, and that the only purpose of the laity was

to support the strata of the pyramid above them. This view of the role of the lay people in the Church has been capsulated in the phrase given in the title of this chapter; the function of the laity is to pray, pay, and obey.

This assumption was not seriously and radically questioned by bishops and pastors within the Church—nor even by the lay people themselves. But once again, the Second Vatican Council planted a bomb under this assumption and the bomb had a short fuse. Lay people, in the United States and in almost every country where Roman Catholicism has a large membership, are praying liturgically rather than largely through their private devotions; they are continuing to pay generously, but are increasingly talking of picketing through their pocket books where, in their opinion, bishops and priests are failing to live up to the spirit and even the letter of the Second Vatican Council. Nor are they obeying in the way which had marked their previous response to the voice of religious authority. Many lay people have taken seriously the statement of The Second Vatican Council that the Church "is the people of God on pilgrimage," rather than a well-disciplined army on the march. It is most significant, as we pointed out in chapter 5, that the Second Vatican Council turned the spotlight on the forgotten church, the lay person, and gave laymen and laywomen more attention and concern than was given either to priests or to nuns. For a Protestant, it might be interesting to notice that the Council, in eight separate places, speaks in detail of *the priesthood of the laity*. For centuries, Protestants have felt that this was one of the concepts basic to Protestantism; precisely because Protestants valued the priesthood of all believers so highly, Roman Catholicism chose to regard it as a toadstool rather than a mushroom and deliberately ignored this immensely significant theological concept. Taking his directives from the Second Vatican Council itself, the Catholic lay person can now understand his role in the Church—one of full participation in its life and mission—as flowing from his sharing, as a lay person, in the priesthood of Christ.

To some Catholics, of course, the phrase "the priesthood of the laity" causes a reaction of surprise. To others hearing it, it may even bring something close to a feeling of shock. To others, fortunately a very few, the phrase may bring a cynical reaction, as though it were merely a glittering, but meaningless, metaphor.

There is, however, in the phrase "priesthood of the laity" and more importantly, in the reality behind the phrase, nothing which should surprise, nothing which should shock and, least of all, nothing to give grounds for cynicism. For the phrase and the reality behind the phrase are literally as old as Christianity itself. St. Peter was talking to his entire Christian community, and not to its ordained ministers alone, when he reminded the members of his flock that they were "a kingly nation," "a royal priesthood," whose vocation it was to proclaim the marvelous deeds of God Who called them out of the darkness into his ineffable light.

Centuries later, St. Augustine, fingering the same theme, told the members of his flock that the name of "priest" belonged to all, because the tasks of the priesthood fell upon all. And many centuries later, Pius XII declared that the laity should be informed of their priesthood, and that the fact of their priesthood should neither be minimized nor denied. It is obvious, then, that when we attempt to learn more about the priesthood proper to the Catholic layman and laywoman, we are not dealing with either dangerous subtleties or trivial novelties. We are, rather, thinking with the mind of the Church as that mind has expressed itself at the highest level, from the times of the earlier Christians down to our own present.

If we are, then, to explore what is actually involved in the Catholic understanding of the priesthood of the laity, we must ask first what accounts for the fact of this priesthood, and secondly, what are its functions.

The fact of our priesthood stems from the most momentous fact in our lives, namely, that at a given time, in a given place, we received the sacrament of Baptism. One way of expressing the reality of Baptism is to say that through this act, and by this fact, we entered the Church. As we saw in chapter 4, perhaps an even more illuminating way of expressing the reality of Baptism is to say that through Baptism we became members of Christ's Mystical Body, that we were incorporated into Christ, that we became one with Him. And if we have been made one with Christ and thereby live with His life as members of His Mystical Body, then there falls upon us the responsibility of attempting to fulfil the yet unfinished tasks of Christ, the great High Priest. This staggering reality lies behind the thought of St. Thomas Aquinas, for example, when he proclaims that Baptism is a participation in the very priesthood of Christ.

We are, then, in no way minimizing either the sacred character or the special responsibilities of the consecrated priest, the ordained minister of God, when we say that for the lay member of the Church his very Baptism was, in effect, also an ordination.

Granted, then, the fact of our priesthood as a consequence of our incorporation into Christ, we must ask, quite bluntly, what difference this fact makes, or should make, in our lives. What is expected of us, what obligations weigh upon us, as a direct consequence of the priesthood of the laity? Wherever we find the institution of the priesthood—among peoples no matter how seemingly primitive or seemingly sophisticated—we find that the priest is expected to discharge at least two functions: he is to be a mediator between God and man, and he is expected to offer sacrifice. It is no different with ourselves. As "lay priests" (and we can now see that this phrase is in no way a contradiction) we, too, are called upon to discharge the priestly tasks of *mediation* and *sacrifice*.

Perhaps the easiest way to understand what is meant by priestly mediation is to recall an old Roman word for a priest. One of the ancient names for a priest, from which we derive our term "pontiff," is the Latin word, *pontifex*. This word means, literally, "a bridge builder." What, then, is a priest? He is a bridge builder, standing, as it were, between God and man with one arm reaching out to each; his task, precisely as a priest, is both to build and to be a bridge, making it easier for man to go to God and easier for God to come to man.

In the Catholic institution of the priesthood, the consecrated priest performs this task of bridge-building in a specifically supernatural context. He is empowered to proclaim and to preach the Word of God; he is "the steward of God's mysteries." He is the ordinary minister of most of the Sacraments; he is to give spiritual counsel and direction.

But the great task of priestly mediation—of bridge-building between God and man—cannot be done completely or exclusively by the ordained priest, for the ordained priest does not usually function as a priest in my office, or my factory, or my home, or in my places of recreation and amusement. And yet there are bridges to be built in all of these places, bridges which only I can build. For Christ wishes to be present in all these places, and He can be there only if I bring Him there. Christ wishes to be present in the place where I work, and He can be present there through me if I attempt to think the Christlike thought, speak the Christlike word, do the Christlike act. We Christians must remind ourselves that in an age of growing religious skepticism and doubt, when Christianity itself seems to be on trial, I may be the only copy of the Gospels which many of my friends and acquaintances will ever read, that they will either know the life of Christ through my life or will not know it at all.

And Christ wishes, too, to be present at my places of recreation. There is the task of mediation to be done at the beach, at the bowling alley, at the cocktail party—a task of mediation which the consecrated priest is not necessarily called upon to perform, and yet a task of mediation which Christ wants done. But the greatest task of priestly mediation for the layman lies, of course, in the temple of his home.

We who are parents love our children with a deathless love. For them we would make any sacrifice, including that of life itself. But is this really enough? Are not these qualities of love and self-sacrifice the natural virtues of parenthood, for does not even the good pagan feel thus and act thus? For us who are Christians, something more is demanded. We are to be parents toward our children but, even more importantly, we are to be priests toward them, bridge-builders. By what we are and by what we do, far more than by what we say, we are expected to make it easier for our children to move to God and to make it easier, in our human terms, for God to come to them.

We who are husbands and wives love our spouses with a deathless love. We would make any sacrifice, including that of life itself, for our beloved. But is this really enough? Does not even the good pagan husband and wife feel thus and act thus, for these qualities of love and sacrifice are the natural virtues of wedded love.

But we who are joined to each other in Christian marriage have each administered to the other the Sacrament of Matrimony. Certainly, from us, something more is demanded. What is demanded is that we be toward each other not only husband or wife, but priest. Thus, far more by what we are and by what we do than by what we say, we are expected to build a bridge between our partner and God, making it easier for him or her to move to God and making it somewhat easier, in our human terms, for God to come to our beloved.

The second great task of the priest is to offer sacrifice and hence, it becomes our task, too, in virtue of that priesthood which is ours. It is unfortunate that the very word "sacrifice," has taken on for us the suggestion of the unpleasant, the difficult, the irksome—that which we would really rather not do, but which we do from a sense of duty.

But the word "sacrifice" need not mean only the irritating, the unpleasant, the cross to be borne. As St. Augustine reminds us, the term means literally "that which has been made holy," and something is made holy if it is offered to God.

This means that we can offer to God as an acceptable sacrifice everything in our lives, except sin. It means, then, that there is, and should be nothing trivial in our lives, nothing irrelevant, nothing unimportant. For everything in our lives can take on an eternal resonance and timeless significance because it has been offered to God in praise, in reparation, in petition, in thanksgiving.

And the Catholic lay-priest obviously performs this necessary task of offering sacrifice most completely and most effectively through the Sacrifice of the Mass, wherein he is called upon to be, not a spectator, but a participant. For in the Mass, I, as one individual, join not only with the congregation, not only with the priest, but with the entire Church in offering God to God. So important is participation in the Mass, so indispensable to discharging the priestly task of offering sacrifice, that each Catholic might well consider whether he does not have the privileged responsibility of sharing in the Mass daily if possible—not if merely convenient, not so long as it is emotionally satisfying—but, if possible.

This, then, is the most important single explanation of why the changes in the Church are taking place not only through the bishops, the ordained priests and the nuns, but through the laity as well. The natives who live at the bottom of the pyramid are restless, because they have now been told that they, too, are not only first-class citizens in the kingdom but are priests as well.

It is in discharge of their priestly tasks, their mediation not only to the world but to other members of the Church, that they have formed their own associations. In this discharge they have demanded a share in the policy-shaping and decision-making of the Church. They have generally made considerable noise and have, on occasion, resisted Church authority where the decisions of that authority did not recommend themselves as reasonable or, indeed, fully Christian.

It could, of course, be understood here that I am speaking only of "liberal" Catholic lay people; I am not. For almost every group of lay people who support priests in conflict with their bishops, there is a corresponding group of lay people who support the bishop against the priest. Where there are groups of lay people

insisting that even further changes be made in the liturgy to have
it more meaningful and relevant, there is to be found a group of
lay people championing the "old way of doing things"—they
would, in effect (and I say this with all respect) like to pray, pay,
and obey in the manner to which they were taught prior to the
Council.

The number of such "conservative" Catholic lay people is
presently large, but is incapable of future growth. They are, for
the most part, of middle age and beyond and the future is not in
their hands. The future belongs to the young in heart, which is a
description of temperament rather than chronology. And the young
at heart have responded, not only with sometimes strident enthusiasm, but also with a quiet commitment to their priesthood. As a
consequence, the basement of the house has become in part a
caucus room and one of the major places "where the action is."
There is no longer an inert broad base to the pyramid.

Lay trustees now form the major governing bodies of a number
of America's most prestigious universities, such as Notre Dame,
Fordham, Georgetown, and St. Louis. In addition, laymen and
women are presidents of a number of American Catholic colleges
where, until a decade ago, it was felt that a lay person was
absolutely unqualified to teach theology, and could teach philosophy only under close surveillance.

In addition, truly representative boards of education have been
set up in more than twenty dioceses throughout the United States,
and lay people have both active and passive voices on these
boards. Most of the major Catholic journals and newspapers are
either edited by laymen or have laymen and women in responsible
positions on their editorial staffs. We have already referred to the
international Congress of the Laity, which informed the Pope, at
its meeting in Rome, of its position on birth control months before
Humane Vitae was issued. After the promulgation of this encyclical, most of the members informed the Pope that the encyclical
had not changed their point of view. The laity are also represented, in proportionate numbers, on diocesan senates and parish

councils, as well as on official Catholic committees dealing with racial equality, urban problems, and international justice. Indeed, the small, select Vatican Commission for World Peace and Justice numbers among its members six women, including the internationally recognized economist, Barbara Ward.

I remember this basement well. It was always a rather busy place, but so often the activities that took place here were mere tasks, busy work. These were considered all that the laity was capable of: running the cake sale, conducting the weekly or monthly fund-raising activities, and in general assuring the shepherd that the sheep were contented. The basement will, of course, never be the same again. Most lay people whom I know, even though now beset with committee meetings, reports, and even protests, prefer their quarters the way they are now—occasionally noisy, but electric with purposeful excitement and alive with activity appropriate to the high calling of the Priesthood of the Faithful.

We have been drawing several similarities between the tasks of the ordained minister—the consecrated priest—and that of the priesthood proper to the layman. There is yet a further similarity —and one which we must take most seriously: just as the consecrated priest does not dare to assume the burdens of his vocation without a long preparation of prayer and study, so too, the responsibilities of the lay priesthood demand the preparation of prayer and study.

Never, in the entire history of the Church, has the layman had spread out before him such opportunities as we enjoy to know Christ and to investigate even more deeply the riches of His revelation. Nor has the layman ever, in two thousand years of Christian history, had such opportunities to form a Christian attitude toward the moral demands of his own time.

The Catholic lay person is now free to move about the house. It is a thrill for him to leave the basement, and spend more time in an airier, sunlit portion of his house—the room we will visit **next**.

9

The Library

Before we enter, might we stand just a moment in the doorway and look around this large and graceful room? You will notice that the last of the heavy, damask drapes is being removed from the large window on the left. The sunlight streams in and calls into life the rich colors of the books, and picks up the glint of the gold and the silver lettering on their bindings. All in all, it looks rather like a modern library should—a learning center, bright, with a view through the spacious uncurtained windows onto the world beyond, inviting in its warmth and color.

Our library did not always look this way. Indeed, until a few short years ago, it was a rather drab, depressing place. The windows were curtained then, and even in daylight one had to depend on the rather weak illumination that came from the anachronistic chandeliers. Whole portions of the library could be entered only if one had a special pass from the head librarian—a pass which indicated that the bearer had sufficient training in Roman Catholic theology to read, without damage to his faith, the writings of Protestant, Jewish, or atheistic thinkers in the fields of religion, ethics, and Church history. I am referring, of course to the famous Index of Prohibited Books— a feature of Roman Catholic life which was known to almost every non-Catholic, and which caused Catholics endless hours of explanation as they attempted to defend the indefensible.

The Index was a strange creation, indeed. It came into being

shortly after the Protestant Reformation; its purpose was to give
warning to Catholics of books which might "endanger their Faith"
or distort their moral perspectives. I suppose that good arguments
could be made to support the creation of such an Index, particularly if one recalls that the majority of Roman Catholics in the
post-Reformation period were comparatively uneducated. The fact
that so many, however, could scarcely read anything makes the
more remarkable the Church's official concern lest they read
works of non-Catholic theology and moral philosophy—works
which the average Catholic, even in our own day, would pass by
in preference for the sports page or a good who-done-it.

As a consequence, the Index was like a fence keeping in precisely those who had every right to graze in other pastures—
serious students and, indeed, scholars in the fields of theology and
philosophy. When a law has eventually proved its ridiculousness,
then there arise greater dangers than those the laws sought to
prevent: either a contempt for law itself, or routinized ways of
getting around the bad laws in question, or, lastly, a rather desperate effort, on the part of the guardians of the law, to prop up the
bad law with rotting timbers.

We are, of course, familiar with this kind of reaction to bad
i.e., unenforceable laws, in the case of prohibition, or the laws
which attempt to eliminate prostitution. The Roman Catholic
has also experienced the unfortunate consequences of bad law in
the case of the Church's legislation concerning the Index of Prohibited Books.

I mention the following facts, not to poke fun in a cheap way
at the Index, any more than one should poke cheap fun at the
Eighteenth Amendment. Both pieces of legislation were brought
into being by sincere and not unintelligent legislators, concerned
with moving against what they saw to be "a clear and present
danger" to the well-being of the community for which they had
the responsibility of enacting laws. Galileo's treatise on the movement of the earth was, however, placed on the Index within the
author's lifetime, and was never removed. *The Count of Monte*

Christo by Alexander Dumas was placed upon the Index because it seemed to support the suggestion that a duel of honor was not sinful, even though such a duel violated the spirit, and often the letter, of the commandment, "Thou shalt not kill." The first English novel, *Pamela,* by Samuel Richardson, was also placed on the Index for its sexual suggestiveness, although even coeds today, required to read *Pamela* in literature classes, can course through the adventures of this hapless maiden without a blush.

There may have been understandable historical reasons why each of these works had been placed upon the Index; it is hard to find, however, a rational explanation for the fact that once a work was placed upon the Index, it seemed impossible to remove it. It seemed, indeed, as though the Index of forbidden books was less a printed document and more like a granite tablet, from which an inscription could be removed only with the greatest difficulty.

The fact that the Index—a piece of serious legislation—was not really seriously administered by Roman authorities led to situations far more harmful than the effects of reading *Pamela,* or *The Count of Monte Cristo* could ever be, not to mention, of course, the reading of Galileo. The legislation itself became increasingly ignored and, when honored at all, was honored in a merely legalistic manner. I have attended Catholic colleges and universities, and have myself taught in three of them. Over that span of years, I have never seen a copy of the Index of Prohibited Books, nor am I sure that the library at any of these Catholic centers of learning even possessed a copy.

The Index has now been abrogated officially by the Roman Catholic Church. The abrogation came not a century too soon, and I know of no reading Catholic who shed a tear at the passing of the Index. The Index was abrogated in part because its legislation was practically unenforceable (if the Church were to attempt to put on the Index every morally objectionable novel today, for example, a supplement to the Index would have to be published every week). But the Church had also come to a new understanding of the intellectual tradition of Christianity. It is for this reason that the drapes which once kept sunlight from this room have been removed, that the locks have been taken from some of the grilled shelves, and that the whole room has taken on a new and bright appearance. It might be well for us both to reflect, at least briefly, on what this recovered understanding of the Catholic intellectual tradition and the "meaning of a library" actually entails for all of the Christian Churches.

A library is a living repository of the living past. But a library is, of course, much more than a link to the past, vital though the uses of the past are to our present needs. A library must also mirror in itself the present—and mirror it fully and accurately, or it becomes a museum and should, in the interests of honesty, be so named.

A library, then, is not only placed in the present, but must be responsive to the present, even while it offers us a link to the vital, the irreplaceable, past. And because the library brings together in one place both the present and the past, the *now* and the *was,* it becomes a womb of the future, an agent of the *what-will-be.*

But a library, for the Christian, is even more. Like a chapel, it represents, in our Christian intellectual tradition, a sacred space. *"Res sacra, homo."* Man is a sacred being, and all the works of his hands, his head, his heart are—or can be—holy. The Christian intellectual tradition is amazingly broad, and surprisingly sensitive to every nuance of the human mind. If one were to flip through the pages of history to find an authentic expression of this Christian intellectual tradition, he would find it first expressed in memorable and irrevocable terms by Origen, one of the greatest figures of the Patristic Age. Origen, as you recall, was one of the first teachers in the first Christian school known to history. This school was established in Alexandria late in the second century, when Alexandria held the world's most famous library and was the cultural and intellectual center of the world.

In this first Christian school, Origen did not warn his students against the wisdom of the pagans, nor was the famous library of Alexandria declared off limits. Strongly to the contrary, Origen stipulated that his students were to avail themselves to the full of the riches that Alexandria offered to the youthful mind, and insisted that his Christian students be exposed to the whole range of traditional Greek liberal education.

"For," said Origen, "these studies will be of no small help to the students in their study and understanding of the Scriptures." Thus Origen, a Christian intellectual, at the dawn of the third century broke the old iron circle of Greek humanistic studies. These studies had been deemed by centuries of Greeks and Romans as the core of *liberal* education, that befitting the *free* man, the privileged; yet Origen saw these same studies as a preparation for the study of the Gospels which present to man's astounded gaze a portrait of the Incarnate Word, "who took upon Himself the form of a slave," the Son of Man who had not "whereon to lay his head."

It is significant for this occasion—standing here in the center of a Catholic library—to recall the description of this school at Alexandria given by Gregory, one of Origen's great pupils. "Nothing," he wrote, "was forbidden us, nothing hidden from us, nothing inaccessible to us. We were to learn all manner of doctrine, Barbarian or Greek, mystical or political, divine or human. We went into and examined with entire freedom all manner of ideas, in order to enjoy to the full these goods of the mind. When an ancient thought was true, it belonged to us, and was at our disposition with all its possibilities of delightful contemplation."

This search for an all-inclusive knowledge, as described here by Gregory, represented at the same time a yet more demanding task—the task, as he expressed it, "of subsuming all these truths under the Holy Word—the loveliest thing there is." For to the Christian and to the Jew, in the ultimate analysis the word "truth," like the word "God," has no plural. And truth for the Christian and for the Jew is, indeed, in the ultimate analysis, a Person, and man's restless search for truth becomes not the play of intellect but the pursuit of a person in love.

This understanding of the life of the mind for the Christian we find caught up from its Patristic origins and woven into the living fabric of the Christian intellectual tradition at its best. We find it, for example, expressed, in the labors of centuries, by the Benedictine monks who bequeathed to us of later generations both the love of learning and the desire of God.

The Benedictine tradition saw no incompatibility between these two human drives, but saw, indeed, each complementing the other. It is this tradition which was caught up and richly embodied centuries later in the work and the life of St. Thomas Aquinas, whose charter for the Christian intelligence might also have been expressed in his dictum that "whatever is true, regardless of who said it, comes from the Holy Spirit."

We today are born of a time which has more information than it can handle but finds wisdom in short supply. Perhaps we need almost daily this reminder of Thomas to his students, that whenever we lay hold of the truth—any truth—we lay hold, no matter how dimly, of the primal Truth Who is a Person and Whose name we know.

When we read, as well as when we pray, we will come to the lived realization that when we discover truth, we discover Christ. An awesome discovery, indeed, because for a Christian to discover Christ is to discover himself, and to make a pledge of himself to what he has discovered. We who follow Him must likewise imitate Him, and He came among men, not to be ministered unto, but to minister; not to be served, but to serve.

The word "service" was a favorite in the documents of the Second Vatican Council. Both the Church itself and the individual Catholic are called upon to serve, even as was the Lord Jesus Himself. The Second Vatican Council thus set an agenda for the last third of the twentieth century; it is only now, several years after the close of the Council, that most Catholics (prelates as well as their people) are beginning to realize the sweep and challenge of the agenda set before us.

One of the most demanding items on that agenda is to be found in the conciliar decree on Ecumenism. This document insists that every Catholic is to think, speak, and act ecumenically, is to make his own the Church's declared intention of striving to regain the lost unity of those who profess "one Lord, one faith, one Baptism."

For very many Catholics, however, this new summons personally to work and pray for Christian unity presents difficulties. They were caught unprepared for this new awareness of, and openness to, the Christians of other churches. Before the Council, most of us could deal with stereotypes of the Protestant, and we felt little need ever to examine whether or not the Protestant really was even remotely what we imagined him to be.

Now the stereotypes are being smashed, and we are forced to search out the authentic features of our Protestant brothers. Understanding must replace the indifference and ignorance which scarred the past; respect and love must displace the suspicion and hostility which were such a scandal to the non-Christian world.

Thousands of Catholics, however, will find it difficult to express this ecumenical dimension in their lives; they must be educated for ecumenism, and for the majority the best and most solid educator will be good books.

We must begin, for example, with the realization that because of our tragic separation, each Christian church has been poorer. Protestants, for example, have historically tended to give the Scriptures a place of central importance, but in their deep concern for "the Sacrament of the Word" neglected, perhaps, the other sacraments. The Catholic Church kept vibrantly alive an understanding of the Christian sacramental life, but neglected the Sacrament of the Word.

We have now begun to realize that each of us is incomplete without the other. Each had thought, in the days of our division, that he was keeping the faith intact behind the wall that separated him from "the others," those Christians who were often called "heretics" and who lived in error and half-truths. Now we are beginning to realize that, on both sides of the wall, the faith suffered distortion precisely because it was kept in isolation. Good fences make good neighbors, but they make for very incomplete theologians.

Every Catholic, then, who would take seriously the high ecumenical mandate of the Council must come to a knowledge of, and respect for, the beliefs and practices of the major Protestant churches. Only in this way can he come to see the wisdom of the ecumenical principle set down by both Pope John and Pope Paul: "to stress what we have in common rather than what divides us." Only by coming to know the Protestant in his deepest beliefs can we come to love him with the genuine charity which ecumenism demands.

Such understanding of Protestants and Protestantism can, of course, be gained through lectures, personal contacts, and discussion groups. For most Catholics, however, the most direct, effective and convenient guide to Protestantism will be a good book, and there are, thank God, a number of such books available today. Any library which does not have a representation of such books can, perhaps, no longer be called a truly Catholic library, since the Council has made it plain that to be a Catholic today is to be ecumenical.

Up to this point, however, we have been discussing ecumenical reading only in terms of what we might call its curative aspects: replacing stereotypes with solid knowledge of the Protestant tradition, and replacing the prejudice of the past with respect and love.

There is an intensely positive side, however, to ecumenical reading; it is, even more importantly, creative as well as curative, and it looks to the future rather than only to the past. Put simply, this positive thrust rests on the fact that theology itself must increasingly be a collaborative, ecumenical effort. The day of the isolated Protestant or Catholic theologian has seen its sunset. The new day is the day of ecumenical theology.

Here are a few obvious examples. No Catholic theologian can any longer discuss papal infallibility without taking into real account what contemporary Protestant theologians are saying about it—and why. No Protestant theologian dare today simply repeat traditional objections to the Catholic theology of the Eucharist, for that theology has developed in depth and clarity precisely in response to Protestant questionings. Nor can either Protestant or Catholic theologians go about their work without paying attention to what some Orthodox theologians call "the Christocentric heresy" of Western Christianity: emphasizing Christ to the point of virtually ignoring the Holy Spirit.

There is evidence all about us that ecumenical theology is not only effective, but is also exciting. A number of major Catholic universities have Protestant and Jewish theologians on their staffs; several Catholic seminaries have coordinated faculty, courses, and libraries with nearby Protestant seminaries, and major Protestant divinity schools have added Catholic theologians to their staffs.

This comparatively recent realization that theology is a shared exploration into the riches of divine revelation has already resulted in a number of stimulating and significant books, without which any Catholic library is measurably poorer.

Theology, of course, is not the whole of the Christian life, important though theology must continue to be. Christianity is more than a collection of doctrines to be believed; it is a set of values to be lived. The vitality and authenticity of the ecumenical movement is to be seen, therefore, not only in the development of an ecumenical theology, but in the development of what is often called secular ecumenism.

By this term is simply meant the common concern of all Christians for "building the earthly city," in the phrase used by the Council in the *Constitution on the Church in the Modern World*.

In the past both Protestantism and Catholicism had trouble fitting the earthly city into their understanding of God's plan. The earthly city, the world, was frequently looked upon as a booby-trapped universe, a source of temptation to the Christian. It was contrasted to the heavenly city, which would endure long after the earthly city had disappeared.

As a consequence, what happened in and to the earthly city was of little concern to the true Christian. Its pleasures and its pain, its splendors and its squalor, were alike ephemeral, and the Christian was to walk through the world with his eyes fixed upon his true, abiding home in the world to come.

Now, however, we Christians have all been made aware that the earth is a global village, and that we bear some responsibility for the quality of life in that village. Brutalizing poverty, the dung heap whereon are spawned hunger, illiteracy, disease, despair, and violence, is not the will of God for His children, but is the product of human blindness and greed.

The Christian can no longer look away from the inhuman squalor of the village, nor sniff the perfumed handkerchief of purely personal piety to keep away the stench of rotten political and social structures. In the strong phrase of John F. Kennedy, "the work of God in the world must surely be our own."

Ecumenism has already begun to flower in common witness and service to the world. On the highest level, the World Council of Churches and the Vatican Commission on World Justice and Peace have begun to pool resources of personnel and money to assist the desperate needs of the so-called emerging nations, which are the homelands of almost two thirds of the world's population.

In a number of major American cities Protestant, Catholic, and Jewish leaders and organizations have begun to work together on the massive problems of the ghettoes, thus replacing with collaboration the older order of wasteful, prideful separate operations on which each carried his own banner into the war against the corrosive enemies of human dignity.

It is also to be noted, gratefully, that the white Christian Churches have recently come awake to the fact that there are, in the United States, millions of black Christians. These had always been safely counted as in the "Christian camp"—much as the Democrats would consider Negro voters in the larger cities as "safe precincts."

The black Christians had their own churches—mercifully removed by blocks or miles from the white church of the same denomination, and were content to preach, in the main, a second-class Christianity to those who already had been made to realize that they were second-class citizens in the land of the free.

But, just as there has been a new demand for "black power" politically, economically, and educationally, so too there has been a sudden insistence on black power within the white Christian establishment—an insistence that Negroes be admitted to the Table of the Lord as equal sharers, who do not need the white man to break for them the Bread which was first given that "all may be one, as thou, Father, in me and I in thee."

The emergence of "black-power" Christian churches—uncomfortable and challenging to those who sit in the comfortable pews of American suburban Christianity—is yet another reminder that the ecumenical age in which we live stands yet at its dawning.

What that day, in its course, will see, what the warmth of its ascending sun will bring to flower, no man can foretell. One thing, however, is certain: the Holy Ghost broods over the ecumenical age with "warm breast and with Ah! bright wings." Many men and women have felt upon their cheeks the rising of this new Pentecostal Wind, and have given us books to enable us to understand what this second coming of the Spirit means—to the churches and their people.

The Wind grows stronger, and there will be more books, the very content of which will be the result of inspiration—the breathing upon man by the Holy Spirit. Our task as Christians is to read with open mind and open heart, and thereby to serve the Spirit of *creative love* which so obviously informs the ecumenical age into which we have been summoned.

10

Dogma and Devotion

You may perhaps have noticed, as we have moved about the house, that in every room, from headquarters to the basement, there has been a statute of the Virgin Mary, and usually, those of one or two other saints. It would probably be a source of relief to you and to me, if I could say, with a wave of the hand, that devotion to Mary and the saints is one aspect of the Church's life which has not been changed by the Council. Unfortunately, I cannot make that sweep of the hand, or utter that remark. Here, too, the Second Vatican Council has had a profound effect on both dogma and devotion, not by denying the one and minimizing the other, but by giving us Catholics a clearer perspective of both.

We have already attempted, in chapter 2, to clear up certain misconceptions of the Catholic Church's theology of Mary in the life of her Son and in the theology of the Church. Mary has never been the object of worship, but she has certainly been honored by Roman Catholics as more deserving than any other human being of religious devotion. What this religious admiration means, we shall attempt to explain in a few moments. But to remind ourselves of how real, and how long, has been the reverence of the Catholic for Mary, we need only recall that most of the great, ancient cathedrals of Europe are named in her honor, along with hundreds of thousands of Catholic churches, shrines, and missionary chapels throughout the world. We must also remind ourselves that denying, or sharply questioning, the significance of

Mary is a rather late development within Protestantism. Martin Luther, for example, wrote of Mary in terms so laudatory that a modern Roman Catholic might well feel a bit uncomfortable in reading him. I would refer, for example, to his *Commentary on the Magnificat,* to cite but one work. John Calvin, too, followed rather than fractured the earlier Christian tradition in his assigning to Mary a unique role in the thinking of the Church and the life of the Christian. Thus, John Calvin defends the traditional Christian teaching up to the point of the Virgin Birth, and also teaches the perpetual virginity of Mary.

The teaching of the Virgin Birth, following the Gospel narratives of Matthew and Luke, understands that Christ was conceived within the womb of Mary through the power of the Holy Spirit, rather than through the generative act of a man. To God, for Whom all things are possible, the conception of Christ as both God and man could have taken place in the normal mode of human conception, with God miraculously endowing the fertilized ovum with divinity. While this could have been done, the Scriptures seem to indicate that it was not done and that Christ was conceived, fully God and fully man, in the virginal womb of his human mother through the inseminating power of the Holy Spirit who in both the Old and the New Testament is regarded as the "fount of life."

Man must, of course, always ponder why God has done what He has done. One of the best statements that I know giving reasons for the Virgin Birth is that of the distinguished Protestant theologian, Karl Barth, who says that Christ's birth of a virgin manifested His true Divinity. The birth was miraculous, it demanded a Divine Agent, it excluded the possibility of Original Sin in Christ, and it impressed upon both Mary and Joseph the meaning and mystery of the Incarnation. All of these, says Barth, are signs pointing to the fact that the Christ of Bethlehem and Nazareth is, indeed, the Son of God.

Later Protestant thought would seem, largely, to be a reaction against what seemed to be—and very often was—a Roman Catholic exaggeration of the significance of Mary—a reaction which took the form, perhaps, of throwing out not only the baby with the bath water but also dismantling the plumbing fixtures as well.

Roman Catholic devotion to Mary stems from the effort to pay her, in human terms, the type of recognition accorded her by God Himself. According to common Christian belief, rooted in the Old Testament anticipation as well as in New Testament narrative, the Triune God had chosen this young Jewish girl to be the mother of the Incarnate Word. Recalling, in this connection, the words of the Nicene Creed, millions of Christians today, Protestant as well as Catholic, profess their belief that Jesus Christ was "conceived by the Holy Spirit, born of the virgin Mary."

What makes the entire event most meaningful to us, however, is not that Mary was chosen by God to be the passive recipient of His divine action, like a vessel into which water is poured. The most remarkable aspect is that God waited upon the choice of the young Jewish girl; she was free to reject or to accept the incredible role to which she was, not forced, but invited. She accepted: "Behold the handmaid (the serving girl) of the Lord; be it done unto me according to Thy Word."

For centuries Christian theologians have pondered the implications of Mary's simple response, and Christians incapable of theologizing have attempted in their lives to imitate Mary's response to God's initiative. The theologians have seen in Mary, not only the mother of Christ, but also the mother of the Church which He established—the Church which was born from His side on Calvary, and brought to its mature responsibility on Pentecost, in the Upper Room where Mary was present with the Apostles.

We have neither the time nor the space to summarize here the historical records which show how often Roman Catholics have viewed Mary through a distorting lens which magnified her by making her seem "larger than life"—more than human.

Nor can we attempt to summarize how, after the Reformation, much of the Protestant tradition also seemed to see Mary through a lens which minified her role in the Christian economy of salvation. It is enough here simply to point out that the Church, through the Second Vatican Council, gave Catholics clear warning against the excesses to which devotion to Mary had sometimes been carried. It also reasserted Mary's role as, not only the mother of Jesus Christ, the Son of God, but also as the second Eve and the mother of the Church. In similar fashion, some of the major Protestant theologians of today—Karl Barth, Paul Tillich, Emil Brunner, and Max Thurian, among others—have been calling for a Protestant positive reevaluation of Mary which would compensate, both in Protestant thought and devotion, for the neglect over centuries. These theologians are saying that the theology of Christ Himself is inseparable from an evangelically based theology of Mary. One of the best summary statements of this "new" Protestant position is that of Dr. Jaroslav Pelikan, the distinguished church historian at Yale University:

The Protestant criticism of Roman Catholic Mariology will not do any more than score debating points until it is accompanied by a positive discussion of the mother of our Lord as viewed from a biblical and evangelical perspective. "Behold," she said, "henceforth all generations will call me blessed." This generation should be no exception. . . .

. . . In any Protestant Mariology (if one may put those two words together) there are two insights that must be included— Mary's significance for Christ and Mary's significance for the Church. . . .

[Protestant theologians] also need to speak of Mary as the prototype of the Christian believer in the Church. The brief description of her career in the New Testament is a summary of the Christian life in its elations and its depressions. Not only must she be a warrant for the true humanity of Christ; her own true humanity must be recaptured. . . .

. . . Not as a semi-divine being, but as an outstanding member of the communion of saints, she is blessed among women.

When Protestants begin to say this out loud in their teaching and worship and not merely to whisper it in their hearts, as most of them indeed do, then they will be better prepared to speak a word of fraternal warning to their Roman Catholic brethren.

It will be noted that Dr. Pelikan, in speaking of Mary as the prototype of the Christian, also referred to the communion of saints, a phrase which occurs in the Apostles' Creed, recited by many major Protestant churches. For many other Protestants, the concept of a communion of saints can be very difficult to understand. They find themselves in the position of Mrs. Albert Einstein when asked if she understood her husband's writings. She replied, "I know the meaning of every word; it's the sentences which elude me."

In similar fashion, some Protestant traditions so emphasize the one-to-one relationship between Christ and the individual that their church itself tends to become a gathering of saved individuals. For other Protestant faith-communities, as well as for the Roman Catholics, salvation (the orientation of one's life to Christ through His grace) is, of course, an individual affair, but one which takes place within and through the community. The Church is the Body of Christ, and we are all His members. This notion of a Body implies that the individual is at once both himself, John or Jane, but also a member of a community, a people. For this type of Christian, the words of Moses are significant; he sprinkled the blood of heifers upon the Israelites to signify the Covenant which God had made with this people. At a Passover meal, commemorating this precise event, Jesus Christ said, "This is my Blood of the New Covenant," indicating that He was forming a new people who would carry His message and bear His name. It is not only the individual Christian who is called, but a people of which the individual is a member.

For this reason, the saints are paid a special reverence. They had in life distinguished themselves not for brilliance of intellect, gifts of personality, or extraordinary attainments of any kind. They had distinguished themselves by doing well what God had wished them to do in the circumstances of their lives. A saint, a "holy one," is precisely the person who is faithful to God's voice in the everyday demands of one's Christian calling. Each of us recognizes that, no matter how simply said, daily fidelity is extremely hard to perform. For this reason, we honor the saints because we feel confident that they have attained the reward of the good and faithful servant of the Scriptures.

Just as we Americans honor the memory of those heroes who have served the American community well—the unknown fallen soldiers as well as the renowned patriots such as Washington, Jefferson, Lincoln and others—so too we honor in Christian memory the saints who have served the community of the Church. Since they were members of this community in life, they have not lost their concern for the community after their death. But we also believe that, having been linked through Baptism and the Eucharist to Christ the Great High Priest, they join Him in Heaven in His mediation before the Father. As the second Adam, the Father of the New Humanity, Christ can now present to His Father the finest flowering of His Redemptive Sacrifice: men and women whose lives found as explanation their whole-souled and single-hearted love and imitation of His Incarnate Word. Prayers are not offered to the saints as though they were rivals to Christ, or substitutes for Him; prayers are offered to Christ through His saints because, after death as in life, they are united to Him as members of His body.

And we, the living, are also members of the Mystical Body, baptized, as were the saints in heaven, into the death and resurrection of Jesus Christ. Since we form one Body, we are bound together with a unity even closer than that which unites the members of a human family. We believe, then, that the saints remain interested in each of us, and are capable of interceding, with Christ, for us before the Throne. The saints—the unknown millions who are in heaven, as well as those who have been formally canonized and are called saints—constitute with us those whom Christ has redeemed, and Whom he presents to His Father.

The saints in heaven and we, the living upon earth, are also joined in the Mystical Body with the souls in Purgatory. Catholic belief in Purgatory, although it rests scripturally only on a passage in Maccabees, represents a theological development from the early practice of the Christian church; praying for the dead that they might be loosed from their sins. Heaven represents, essentially, the "beatific vision" wherein the saved look upon the Triune God "face to face." Not all who die in the Lord possess the purity of soul requisite for this gazing in complete love and happiness upon Divinity. Purgatory, as the name suggests, is a state of purification wherein what might remain of selfishness in the departed souls is cleansed away. Despite the exaggerations in popular literature and even in preaching, the Church has never officially taught that Purgatory is, as it were, an annex to Hell, differing from it only in the fact that whereas Hell was everlasting, Purgatory was temporal. We do not know the nature of the purification in Purgatory. Since the essence of sin is turning from the Creator toward a creature, thereby preferring one's own will to God's will, some major theologians have suggested that Purgatory "purifies" through love. After death, when all illusion falls away, the soul realizes the infinite lovableness of God. Prevented by its past disposition to love self on occasion more than God, it finds itself "suffering the pangs of not possessing the One it now completely loves." It is the type of suffering with which humans are familiar when they are unable to be in the presence of those who mean more to them even than themselves.

The Catholic Church also teaches that one can atone for past sin and attack the roots of sinfulness—self-love—while yet on earth. The practice of penance, the repeated efforts, no matter how unsuccessful, to grow in love of God and bring death to "the old man" within us can all assist the individual to prepare more adequately for the moment of death. Some contemporary Catholic theologians, taking their cues from contemporary Protestant theologians and philosophers, are also developing a theology of death which suggests that the moment of death represents a final option. In other words, no matter how near death the person may seem to a physician, theologically there would be a moment in which the dying person was given, as throughout his life, the choice between good and evil, between God and selfish love.

We can point out here that the Catholic Church, in dealing with Purgatory, very often conceived it in purely spatial and temporal terms. As a consequence, Purgatory was frequently presented as though it were, in effect, a debtor's prison wherein one was condemned to remain for a period of time until complete satisfaction had been made. We are recovering, as are Protestants, an awareness that God is more a loving Father than a vengeful Judge.

But not everyone learns in his lifetime, as did the prodigal son, fully to appreciate the beauties of his Father's house. It would be more accurate, for this reason, to depict Purgatory as a school of love, wherein one grows in his ability to receive the beatific vision. Many places and many voices in the New Testament remind us that we are to "bear one another's burdens." This obligation does not cease when a member of our community has died. We believe that through our prayers we can assist all of those (how few or many they may be) who are in this state of assured hope, expectation, and unfulfilled love.

We have already referred, a few pages earlier, to the fact that the Christian can prepare himself through life for that moment which will be its most significant one, the moment of his death. In the Catholic view, a significant way in which the Catholic can thus prepare himself is through the Sacrament of Penance. Just as the Catholic believes that Christ empowered his Apostles and their successors in the Church truly to consecrate bread and wine and transform it, through His power, into His Body and Blood, so too the Catholic believes that Christ empowered the Apostles and their successors to forgive sins, not in their name and through their power, but in the name and power of Christ (Matt. 16:19).

It should, perhaps, be immediately pointed out that other Christians as well as Catholics preserve the Sacrament of Penance, which includes making one's confession to an ordained minister. A number of Lutherans and many Episcopalians practice confession, and there has, indeed, been a strengthening rather than a weakening of this practice over the last decade. The theology of the Sacrament of Penance is obviously involved with the theology of salvation. Those Protestants who practice confession, as well as Roman Catholics, believe that salvation is a process; it consists essentially in the life of grace, the sharing with God of His own divine life. This state of union with God can be broken or weakened by the decision of the human partner. We have said earlier that sin represents, in its dark essence, the turning away from God in order that I might turn toward something or someone other than God, that is, choosing an idol rather than the Ineffable Godhead. In effect, then, the sinner is a sinner precisely because he has preferred his will to God's will.

Such a choice can involve a deliberate rejection of God and a severing of the ties which bind us to Him. This Catholics have traditionally called mortal sin precisely because it closes off, by the sinner's choice, the divine life within him. Or the choice between God and a creature may be less definitive, as when one yields to uncharitableness in thought, speech or act, or yields to momentary anger. Whether the bond between God has been severed or merely weakened, the Catholic believes that he can show toward God his sincere repentance by making use of the Sacrament of Penance and, through confession, either restoring or strengthening the bond. Through an act of faith in the Promise of Christ conveyed to His Church, the penitent believes that in confessing his sins to a fellow human being he is nevertheless confessing his sins and expressing his sorrow to Christ himself. Since Christ has, however, appointed men to act as judges in His name, it is necessary for the human judge with supernatural powers to know whereon he is to pass judgment. For this reason, the penitent must mention his sins, certainly those which he considers mortal and whichever lesser sins he cares to confess. We have already pointed out, in the first chapter, that it is not easy, even in the anonymity of a darkened confessional where neither priest nor penitent can see each other, to reveal the sad burden of one's sins and faults, to indicate how often one has betrayed the love and mercy of God. The very effort to do so, however, is a sign of one's sincere remorse and his resolve to attempt, at least, to improve upon his sorry track record in the future.

Occasionally, the task is not made easier by the priest on the other side of the dark grill. He may be, for the moment, out of sorts as a result of problems on his mind or an upset stomach. He may also, at the time one enters the confessional, be already cramped, weary of human frailty and physically tired from having already sat for hours in the confessional listening to the less lovely side of human beings. Or, again, he might simply be a chronically impatient person. None of these dispositions, however, affects the validity of his absolution, even though it may make a bit more difficult the penitent's performance of his job—the honest recounting of his sins, and the pledge of his intention to better his response to God's loving mercy.

On this point, it is well for the Catholic to remind himself that Christ, Who knew what He was doing, chose as His Apostles some strange types indeed. There was Peter, the impetuous, James and John, the "Sons of Thunder," presumably a nickname gained by their short tempers, Thomas, the doubter, and in general, a group of ill-assorted men not above self-seeking and ambition. Yet it was precisely to these men that Christ committed the power to forgive or to withhold forgiveness, and I suspect that many of the Apostles were less easy to approach in making one's confession than have been the overwhelming majority of the priests to whom I have made mine. Nevertheless, almost any Roman Catholic would smile in recognition at the following anecdote given in a recent issue of *Reader's Digest:*

"In Southeast Asia a tent was being used as a chapel, and five lines of soldiers had formed for the five chaplains who were hearing confessions. From behind one curtain came the incredulous voice of a chaplain asking, '*You did what?*' A long moment of silence followed; then a soldier stepped from behind the curtain and hurried out.

"Almost immediately that line of soldiers melted into the other four lines."

Obviously, this particular chaplain was a spiritual descendant of St. James and St. John, the "Sons of Thunder." Even the Pope, however, goes to confession and goes quite frequently. This fact is known because the names of the confessors of the last several popes are matters of public knowledge, and even the greenest Vatican reporter knows how often the Pope's confessor is seen entering Vatican City.

This last point brings up an aspect of confession which is frequently overlooked by many. In addition to serving as a judge, the confessor also serves as a spiritual guide and counselor. I would suspect that in most confessions heard by the average priest, the latter function occupies more of his time than the former. The confessional is no substitute for the psychiatrist's consulting room; but for those Christians who are doing well and would hope to do better, the confessional is a place where they can readily receive not only spiritual direction but also encouragement—a commodity which most of us need and which is, in the world around us, in chronically short supply.

As in almost every other area of Catholic life, however, the Sacrament of Penance and the practice of regular confession is undergoing reevaluation. Catholics are now beginning to realize that they might, in their concentration upon confession, have tended to scant the other ways in which sins less than mortal are forgiven. The Catholic is enjoined to examine his conscience each day, and to make an Act of Contrition for his failings and sins. At the beginning of each Mass, as we have seen, both priest and people confess their sinfulness, and each prays for the other's forgiveness. Before the reading of the Gospel passage in each Mass, both the priest celebrant and the congregation pray that, through the words of the Gospels, their sins may be blotted out.

Each of these situations has served to reinforce the developing recognition within the Catholic Church that one's sins and failings affect not only his own relationship to God, but have also an impact upon the community of which he is a part. For this reason, Catholics in many sections of the Church are employing a scriptural ceremony of repentance similar to that used in many Protestant Churches. Here the community, as a community, acknowledges its sinfulness and failure adequately to respond to God's initiatives of loving invitation. After a silent examination of conscience, each individual then joins with the prayerful assembly in begging God's pardon, and promising a renewed effort to live up to the demands of the Christian calling. The entire ceremony is expressed in word and concepts drawn from both the Old and the New Testaments, and serves to deepen the Church's realization that no matter how splendid the Church is through the love of its Founder, it yet remains in terms of its human members a "Church of sinners."

Neither our attempt to explain what confession means to the Catholic, nor this brief indication of shifts in awareness regarding the many dimensions of the Sacrament of Penance are intended to deny or minimize what has been, for centuries, a tendency among Roman Catholics generally: a certain legalism, a concentration upon the Sacraments as a spiritual medicine chest, a readiness to value more the letter of the law than its spirit. Perhaps we have reached a point in our discussion where we should attempt a kind of rough analysis of the Catholic experience which may enable us to understand more easily both the monochromatic past and the kaleidoscopic present. This we shall attempt in the next chapter.

11

Code or Commitment?

Under the date of November 28, 1968, major Catholic newspapers carried the following report emanating from the National Catholic News Service:

Milwaukee—The publisher of a controversial newspaper said here Catholics are developing "new concepts as to what is right and wrong," and the new life-style of "moral decision-making" is occurring in what is a "shift" from Church authority to individual conscience.

Donald J. Thorman, publisher of *National Catholic Reporter,* discussed the Church's new morality before an audience of priests at a lecture last week at St. Francis Seminary here. "Catholic moral theology has seen in public practice, and to some degree in theory also, a 360-degree turnabout, which, I suspect, has left most Catholics confused, bewildered, and perhaps a little resentful," Thorman said.

Mr. Thorman was basing his observations on a survey which he himself had conducted involving 365 "selected members of the laity." By any professional standard, this would be a very weak sampling of American Catholic opinion, since there are more than 40 million Roman Catholics in the United States. Realistically, however, Mr. Thorman need hardly have surveyed even those 365. The evidence for a bewildering reversal of Catholic moral attitudes is to be found in those groups of priests, nuns, and lay people whom we have seen before, picketing and protesting against what they judge to be the arbitrary, uninformed decisions of ecclesiastical authorities.

Once again, in order to understand the present, we must step back and take a brief look at the past. In this chapter, then, we shall attempt a quick review of the history of moral attitudes within Roman Catholicism—attitudes which had endured for centuries, and which are beginning to crack and crumble now under the pressure of what is happening within and without Roman Catholicism. We have a great deal of ground to cover in a very short time. The trip will be fast and bumpy; for anyone wishing to take it, I would advise buckling seat belts, and holding on to any solid object available.

The history of Moral Philosophy and Moral Teaching demonstrates that morality seems, almost by some inner force, to divide into two basic types. Whether we are concerned with the moral teaching of a Confucius or of a Socrates, we can distinguish between morality *taught as commitment* and *morality practiced as a code.*

Morality viewed as a code stresses the note of *obligation;* it is primarily concerned with the individual act, and seeks to determine whether that individual act is morally good or morally evil. Given the preoccupation of code morality with the goodness or badness of the individual action, it is all but inevitable that it would focus on the question of *sin.* In specifically Catholic terms, therefore, it views the aim and end of moral striving to be that of remaining in the state of grace, or of regaining that state if it has been lost by deliberate, serious sin.

Morality viewed as commitment, on the other hand, strikes the essential note of an *orientation* of the whole being, rather than an obligation to do good or avoid evil. Morality as commitment is thus more concerned with the intention of the actor than with the act itself. Rather than viewing the essential moral choice as being the choice between good and evil, it tends to posit the moral imperative as being the choice of the greater good among the various goods offered to the option of the moral agent. As a consequence, morality as commitment is more concerned with *perfection* than with sinfulness or sinlessness. It views the aim and end of moral action to be *growth in grace,* in Christian terms, rather than viewing remaining in or regaining the state of grace as the essential moral problem.

From even such a brief description of these two fundamental moral perspectives, it will be readily understood why morality as code has been generally thought to be the type of morality suitable to "the masses," while morality as commitment, as an orientation of the whole being toward perfection, is thought of being an ethics of the "elite."

Within Roman Catholicism both types of morality—morality as code and morality as commitment—have been taught, and fostered. But even while recognizing the coexistence, as it were, of these two types of morality within the household of the Faith, we can note a significant difference. Morality as commitment, as the pursuit of perfection, as orientation of the total human being toward the good has been largely concentrated within the religious orders. The call to perfection, the invitation to grow in grace, has been largely linked to the vocation of the professed religious, to the person who voluntarily assumes the responsibilities of the vows of poverty, chastity, and obedience in order to follow what Catholic ascetical writers have for centuries called the "higher way."

Morality as commitment, as orientation toward perfection, has thus been proposed as possible to a chosen few, rather than being persuasively imposed upon the many. The very notion of perfection in the Christian life has involved, in the history of Roman Catholicism, the development of an ethics of an elite.

Even the most superficial acquaintance with the history of religious orders and congregations within Roman Catholicism will recognize how extremely rich this development has been. Think of some of the outstanding founders of religious orders—Benedict, Ignatius Loyola, Francis of Assisi. We are instantly reminded of how central a contribution such leaders have made to the moral awareness and higher morality of Roman Catholicism. And think of the great mystics, such as John of the Cross or Theresa of Avila. These great religious reformers deepened and developed the possibilities for perfection to be found within the seeming restrictions and actual freedoms of the religious community wherein are borne the sweet burdens of vowed poverty, chastity, and obedience.

What is of interest at this point, however, is not the achievements and contributions of these great heroes and heroines of the dedicated religious life. In so many instances their spiritual teaching, their moral perspectives, their blueprints for perfection have not been made available to those who do not lead the life of the vows. How many students of Benedictine schools and colleges, for example, have ever been meaningfully introduced to the spirit of St. Benedict himself? How many students, of the thousands in Jesuit schools and colleges in the United States alone, have ever been led to an understanding of the remarkable insights of Ignatius Loyola into the meaning of the Christian life? How many have caught even a glimpse of the vital spirit which informed the Constitutions of the Society of Jesus which Ignatius founded?

In how many Catholic schools and colleges—whose primary purpose for existence, in the words of Pius XI, is "to form the true and perfect Christian"—is a formal course ever offered on the spiritual teaching (and hence the moral universe) of such giants of the spirit as Benedict, Francis, Ignatius, John of the Cross, or Theresa?

The fact of the matter is that *their* type of morality—indisputably a morality of commitment, of orientation, of the pursuit of perfection—has been but rarely put forward as being applicable to all Christians.

Consider, for example, the students of our Catholic schools and colleges—economically, intellectually, and culturally an elite. Even to these, a dominantly code morality has been taught, which tends to emphasize an outward conformity to the law rather than an interior embracing of the law through love. In effect, a minimal goal was set forth before these thousands. They were taught to concern themselves in their moral decision and in their spiritual life with the "salvation of their souls," rather than being presented with the maximal goal of moral effort—to know Christ more intimately, to love Him more ardently, and to imitate Him more closely. They have not been enjoined in their religious exercises as well as in their formal courses in religion to "put on Christ," in the phrase of St. Paul. It has been generally assumed, among both teachers and the taught, that the vocation to be *alter Christus,* to be another Christ, is the vocation of the elite, of the priest, or of the religious who lives the life of vowed dedication.

Since only this type of code morality has been taught systematically in Catholic schools, it has come gradually to be considered as *the* Catholic morality so far as the great majority of Christians are concerned. As a consequence, formal Catholic moral education, even at the college level, has run the risk of producing what might, with sad accuracy, be called minimal Christians.

Since we have laid such stress upon ethics—moral understanding in the light of human reason—we have run the risk of producing generations of little Stoics rather than vibrant Christians willing to imitate even the folly of the Cross. It is a fairly common experience of the Catholic educator to encounter, after several years, former students who give every sign of being in their personal lives moral hair-splitters, concerned primarily with whether or not a given action is morally sinful. In classroom and pulpit teachers and preachers have been concerned with the minimal demands of Christianity. They have so stressed the Christian's task as essentially the salvation of his own soul, that we have made possible in the eyes of others a completely negative definition of the Catholic as "a person who cannot." He cannot miss Mass on Sunday, cannot get a divorce, cannot practice birth control, and cannot even see a movie condemned by the Legion of Decency (renamed The National Catholic Office for Motion Pictures) as a brief respite from the rigors of Catholic existence.

That negative definition is obviously a caricature; but can we Catholics also say that through classroom and pulpit we have so imparted an understanding of Christian morality that in the eyes of others a Roman Catholic is readily recognized as one "who hungers and thirsts after justice, who is meek and merciful, who is a peacemaker, who is poor in spirit"?

It has been this preoccupation with sin and personal salvation that has led to a long list of Catholic "thou shalt nots," to a morality centered more on law than on love.

There is another and perhaps even more serious consequence of the fact that the morality proposed to the majority of Christians has been that of a code morality. Since morality as commitment was all but confined to those who lived a life of vowed dedication, as this type of morality developed historically it dwelt almost exclusively on those areas of life which touched the priestly or professedly religious life. Hence it did not give a "higher," maximal moral perspective to those areas of life with which the laity were concerned. The realities in the day-to-day life of the layman and woman were thus not brought into sharp focus as aids or obstacles to the fulness of Christian living. So long as these realities were not occasions of sin, they were deemed morally acceptable and licit.

A few examples may help to clarify this admittedly broad and very abstract statement. We have not, to cite one instance, developed an *authentic* spirituality of marriage, although beginnings of such a spirituality have been made within the past three decades. For centuries, however, we have felt that the spirituality of marriage was all but absorbed in its minimal morality. Its primary purpose of procreation must not be frustrated by unnatural means. Its secondary purpose of "relieving concupiscence" is satisfied by the mutual "rendering of the debt." This technical term, by the way, unwittingly shows how removed sexuality had been from any positive consideration that it might possibly be integrated into the orientation of a man and wife toward God. So far as sexuality is concerned, the life of the celibate priest and religious had long been the paradigm for all Catholics who would seek perfection. Sexuality is to be repressed rather than expressed, to be diverted rather than directed. The Second Vatican Council changed all this, but changed it so suddenly that Catholics were bewildered at now being told they were to live by commitment rather than by code.

Again, such momentous developments in the modern world as the growth of the city, the rise of capitalism, the development of democratic government, and the industrial revolution have all touched the "Catholic in the world" at his inmost being. But so far as a Catholic response to these realities was concerned, the layman received little guidance from those following an ethics of the elite. These realities, after all, did not touch the lives of priest and religious with any real urgency. Consequently, these realities—political, economic, cultural—were deemed "secular," pertaining to the City of Man more than to the City of God.

Thus the layman was left to fend for himself, as it were, in the City of Man. Viewing morality as he did primarily in terms of code and obligation, the layman was able to ask of these secular realities only: "Do they lead to *sin?* What am I *commanded* to do?"

As a consequence, among most laymen a myopia was induced toward the moral dimensions of problems in the political, economic, and social order. As we shall see, the Second Vatican Council laid great stress upon the responsibility of the Catholic toward the world. Unfortunately, the Church before the Council had taught the layman to read only the language of code, not the language of commitment. When the Church now tells Catholics that they must fight for racial justice, support decent jobs, housing, and education for all, and assist the have-not nations, many Catholics mutter that the Church should stay out of politics.

The Council, then, is forcing Catholics—bishops, priests, nuns, and lay people—to rethink what is *essential* to Christian morality. When we begin to rethink our perspectives and programs in this light we are immediately struck with the fact that Christ Himself did not offer His followers a choice between a high and a low road, between first- and second-class citizenship in the Kingdom, between two lawful Christian vocations, one of minimal and the other of maximal requirements.

So far as the distinction we have been using is concerned, our Lord taught a morality of commitment, stressing the choice of the greater good rather than the avoidance of evil as the hallmark of the Christian.

"If any man will come after Me, let him deny himself, take up his cross daily, and follow Me." A reading of Luke and Mark seems to make clear that Christ is here speaking to all, not merely to the Apostles, even as He was speaking to all in the Sermon on the Mount. We have no right to teach the Beatitudes as counsels of perfection, to be opted by a chosen few, when Christ so obviously addressed them to all who would follow Him.

Here, I think, we have come close to the heart of the problem. A growing number of priests, nuns, and lay people—especially those under forty—are seeking moral inspiration more from the Mount of Beatitudes than from Mount Siani. They do not, of course, deny or minimize the Ten Commandments, but they are looking for the positive person-directed, love-centered ethic of the Scriptures.

For Catholics over forty, whether bishops or laity, such an emphasis is unfamiliar and may often seem dangerous. Here is the flash-point between generations, between authority and the freedom to make moral decisions. What the "young" generation is really looking for is the biblical portrait of the true servant of God.

The biblical portrait of the true servant of God is embodied in the scriptural concept of the *anawim*—a Hebrew word which means "people who are humble and lowly." No single phrase, however, could contain all that is suggested by the scriptural understanding of the *anawim* as a religious concept.

To be counted among the *anawim* was to be poor in spirit, certainly, but often poor in fact, as well. And as the poor man senses his utter dependence upon others, so too the man who is poor in spirit is aware to the marrow of his being of his utter dependence upon God.

A sense, then, of one's complete helplessness, coupled with a strong sense of God's omnipotence, characterizes the *anawim,* who stand before God as a child stands before its father. They show a childlike faith, a childlike ability to expect nothing and welcome anything from the hands of the father, a childlike trust in the father's love, even when the father seemed neglectful or even scornful.—Such attitudes marked the saints before Christ—Jeremiah, the psalmists, Isaiah, Zechariah and Elizabeth, Joseph of Egypt, and Joseph of Nazareth.

Mary stands in the long line of the biblical figures who embody the moral greatness of the *anawim.* The concept finds, of course, its most splendid realization in the figure of our Lord Himself, who proclaimed his messiahship in the synagogue at Nazareth in terms that his fellow villagers could not fail to understand. After quoting from the lectionary for the day the Prophecy of Isaiah, "The lame shall walk, the blind see, the deaf hear, and the poor shall have the gospel preached to them," our Lord concluded simply by saying, "This day is the Scripture fulfilled in your hearing." "Learn of me," He was later to say, "for I am meek and humble of heart"—the essence of the *anawim* ideal.

All this may seem commonplace to the point of being trite, but we must remember that the serious study of the *anawim* as biblical man, par excellence, was not undertaken until less than thirty years ago. And it is significant that this effort to understand the inner life of the great heroes and heroines of the Old Testament took place precisely when, and perhaps because, the world was entering into a period of darkness—the era of the rise of dictatorships; the erosion of philosophic and religious verities; a world moving inexorably, as almost everyone foresaw, to the brink of a cataclysmic war. And the study by biblical scholars of the moral meaning of the *anawim* continued in the broken world that the Second World War had left in its wake. Further, the investigation of the *anawim,* far from being complete, is receiving continually more intensive investigation in our own time, which cannot forget the threat symbolzed by either the mushroom cloud or the hunger-bloated bellies of the starving in the streets of major cities throughout the non-Caucasian world.

An understanding of the *anawim* as representing, in effect, the moral portrait of the Christian has immediate relevance for the modern layman. He casts his eye over the world and sees that the modern world has its own moral heroes. He sees in these moral heroes a striking quality: they are in every instance concerned with the plight of the poor and with peace. They struggle to bring light to darkened eyes—to heal the scars of human violence and inhumanity. He sees that the modern world has accepted as its criterion of moral meaning and spiritual grandeur men like Gandhi, Albert Schweitzer, Martin Luther King, Thomas Dooley, and Dag Hammarskjold, who considered himself, in a very real sense, the servant of mankind.

The Church itself, as it shows in its recent conciliar decrees, is becoming once more an *anawim* Church. In closer imitation of Mary its Mother and Christ its Bridegroom, the Church is striving to become poor and serving. Biblical phrases, indeed, and all but quaint. But we know their meaning, in part at least, because a Gandhi and a Martin Luther King have shared this time of the world's age with us, and Dostoevski and Camus, Kierkegaard and Teilhard de Chardin have written for us, even as God has spoken to us through the prophets, and lastly through His Son.

Poor—and serving the poor, who remain the sacrament of Christ's presence among men. The Word of God thunders this message in the ears of the Christian today, and the *young,* in particular, wish to respond as did Abraham, Moses, Mary: "Be it done unto me according to Thy Word." This biblical response of the *anawim* ideal must be the key if there is to be a future for Roman Catholicism—as we shall see in the next chapter.

12

The Church
of the Future

For the past decade adult America has been paying considerable attention to the *young* segment of its population. Much of this attention has been forced upon older generations as the younger ones gave strong and often strident notice that they were on the American scene, and were determined to rearrange part of the landscape. In the early '50's, their elders called youth "the silent generation," bemoaned the seeming apathy of college students, and urged them to "speak up." In the '60's, youth is speaking up, and acting up, to the point where many of their elders wish that youth would retire to the shell of silence which encased them even ten short years ago.

Fear of, and consequent rage against, the impersonalism of modern society and impatience with moral ambiguities—these represent, seemingly, the taut strings which account for much of the hostile and unpredictable actions of that portion of American youth which is in revolt. It would be as unwise to exaggerate the size of that portion of America's young people as it would be disastrous to underestimate its significance. Wherever a culture finds more than a miniscule portion of its young chafing at the system and either questioning or defying conventions which have shaped the lives of their elders, that culture would seem to be moving toward a critical phase of its history.

Perhaps the first point to be suggested in considering American *Catholic* youth and a postconciliar Church is that our young people will not have the same attitude toward the Second Vatican Council as that which most of us older Catholics have felt. For anyone over thirty, the Second Vatican Council did indeed mark a revolution in the Church. On point after point, the revolution came—ecumenism, the liturgy, our attitude toward non-Christian religions, the role of the laity in the Church, and, above all, the Church's new understanding of herself as the People of God rather than as a juridical organization. We were forced to see the Church, under the inspiration of the Holy Spirit, enter into what Pope Paul has called a New Pentecost. That experience, however, is denied to those Catholics who have no memory of what the Church was before the Council. The only Church which they can know with any immediacy is indeed the postconciliar Church— the Church which emerged from the Council.

Consequently, they will be impatient with the ambiguities which we of an older generation accept with equanimity and, indeed, attempt to explain away. Thus we will find little difficulty in accepting the fact that the Council itself, in many places, declared that the Church was to be a serving Church even while we recognize that this ideal is not fully achieved. In area after area of its life, not only in America but in the world, the Church still seems to feel itself called upon not to serve but to be served. Further, we can understand how, in sector after sector, members of the Church on every level have tuned out the clear injunction of the conciliar Decree on Ecumenism that Catholics are to take the initiative in attempting to find new ways in which we might come to know, love, and serve our separated brethren. Mere civility, we know, is not an acceptable substitute for charity, but we will plead that the Council has called for many changes in act and attitude, and that change must not be precipitate. One must be patient, we will say, with the efforts of Catholics to change long-standing and deeply cherished ways of life.

But the younger generation does not view change as many of their elders do. The young have grown up in a world which presented them, literally day by day, with the phenomenon of increas-

ingly accelerated change. In their brief lifetime, the amount of
knowledge mastered by man is almost half again what man had
come to know in the last 150 years. In addition to their experience
of the knowledge explosion, this generation has seen social change
take place with a rapidity comparable to that with which season
follows season as the earth journeys around the sun. Thus they
have seen, in their brief lifetime, the Negro make greater strides
toward freedom than he had made in the century after the Civil
War. They have seen America itself become not only a prosperous
but an affluent society. They have seen that affluent society suddenly discover in its midst the millions of poor whom it had forgotten, much as an advancing army may overlook in its surge
forward the wounded left by the wayside.

Confronted then by the capacity of America to change and
change rapidly, young American Catholics are likely to be rather
impatient. They are not prepared to accept the incapacity or at
least reluctance to change which marks a number of Catholics in
position of authority as well as with those who silently rejoice in
the fact that their religious authorities would seem to view the
new Pentecost as though it were Armageddon. We elders might
label this as an understandable reluctance to change, which we
might explain in terms of cultural lag and human weakness. The
younger generation is likely to consider it mere hypocrisy—and
they may be right. We must expect, I fear, a number of movements in the rather near future which can only fill us with dismay.
The postconciliar Church has thrown its full weight of authoritative encouragement, for example, to the ecumenical adventure.
Consequently, a certain number of younger Catholics, clerical
and lay, will assume that the Council meant what it said and
thus will be quite willing to seek ways and means of ecumenical
understanding and action. Some of their approaches will strike
those holding religious authority as daring and, indeed, dangerous.
The sharing of the Eucharist between Catholics and Protestants
would be but one example of what I have in mind—the willingness of the young to carry the premises of their elders to logical

conclusions. For the older generation to point out to the younger that the conclusions are not logical will be a futile exercise. We have given them much opportunity to see that our understanding of "logical" is frequently hard to distinguish from time-serving or timidity.

The same possibility of the young hustling into action waving conciliar documents is even more ripe in the area of social action. Indeed, almost every instance of the "silenced priests" (and religious) has already involved, as we have seen, the case of a youngish person assuming that the Council was to be taken with deadly seriousness when it spoke of the Christian mission to witness against injustice and for peace.

The raw spot here is the rub between the institution and the individual who feels one of two things. Some feel that because the institution is not bearing adequate witness, they must. Others feel that in so bearing witness, they are simply doing what the institution has said its members must do.

This is the late twentieth century, and we are dealing with the Church of the New Pentecost. That is a highly-charged combination. The Council, on almost every point, has affirmed its whole-souled acceptance of what modern man has won and hopes at his best to be. It proclaims his commitment to freedom within community and the fire in his belly to make of the earth a home and of mankind a family.

This is the only world of human values the young American Catholic either knows or cares about, in the Church or in the world. He has not experienced the nationalism that marked his parents as youthful Americans, or the triumphalism which marked his parents as youthful Catholics. The young—if they care at all —will care about universalism of both Church and world.

To say that, I suspect, is to say that they have already strode past most of us in older generations. When I think of the Peace Corps, or see photos of white college students enrolling Negro voters, or picketing a chancery, or working with VISTA, or demonstrating against the Vietnam War, I feel a pang of shame and envy. In my day, children of the depression though we were and bearing its "invisible scar"—we made intercollegiate competitions of swallowing goldfish or seeing how many we could crowd into a phone booth.

There was mindlessness in us, but little malice. We were the prisoners of our times—until the blasts of World War II shattered the walls and made us see that hells had opened just beyond our gates. Those who are young today cannot be considered prisoners of their time. Their time is a blessed one in which to be baptized and breathing—and young. They live in a society which aspires to be servant of the world as it gropes, no matter how blindly, not only toward the freedoms of man but to the perfect freedom of the sons of God. Their heroes, as we have seen, fit the biblical pattern of the *anawim.*

It is there, I think, that any consideration of youth in the postconciliar Church will find its hinge. Youth will not fail the future unless we of the present generation of priests and parents, teachers and prelates, fail our youth. We must not trim the vision down to our size, nor present to youth the challenge of a serving, pilgrim Church in terms of what our comfort and security wishes that challenge were. We must not attempt to domesticate the Holy Spirit, nor act toward youth as though our well-kept houses and shaded gardens were the modern Church of her frontiers.

Youth is clear-eyed, despite all ancient adages to the contrary, and even to attempt the farce would be to lose the youthful elite we most would care to keep. Unless we try to act as the Christians we tell them to be, we will turn into ineffectual rebels the young revolutionaries which the world needs and which the Church of the Council had tried to form in the womb of prayer and travail.

The consideration of Catholic young people necessarily involves some consideration of the future of Catholic education. It is an obvious feature of the American educational landscape, since at the present time the Catholic school system represents a large part of the total educational picture. For example, Catholic schools exist in every state of the Union. In half of the states, these

Catholic schools educate more than 10 percent of the state's students; in ten states, Catholic schools account for the education of 20 to 25 percent of the total state enrolment. Catholics spend $7,500,000 per day to maintain their schools throughout the nation.

It is obvious that the effort to keep this massive Catholic educational enterprise effective and constantly to improve it, drains the time, energies and finances of the Catholics involved— bishops, priests, nuns, and lay people. It is also becoming increasingly clear that serious questions are being raised. Can the Church in the United States find sufficient funds to maintain its present statistical and academic level? Should it invest so massively in Catholic education from postdiaper to postdoctoral institutions?

Consider first the question of whether or not the Church can continue to face mounting educational costs. It is significant that in a number of major Roman Catholic dioceses throughout the country, a moratorium has been declared on further parochial school construction. In Cincinnati, Rochester, St. Louis, Spokane, and Kansas City, to mention only some, Church authorities, faced with a shortage of teachers and classrooms, have curtailed certain classes and have put aside temporarily any plans for badly-needed expansion. It should also be pointed out that this decision was made the more painful because Catholic parents continue to support their parochial schools. The money has not run out, nor has the steam escaped from Catholic education because parents have abandoned the desire to have their children receive a Catholic education. A spot check made in the summer of 1968 reveals that, in ten dioceses alone, almost fifty thousand applicants were turned away because of a shortage of teacher and classroom facilities. The desire for Catholic education is there on the part of parents and prelates. What is lacking is precisely what is lacking in so much public education at the moment—adequate funds to meet the educational needs of a rapidly expanding student population.

What about the advisability of continuing the Church's massive educational efforts, particularly on the elementary school level? In the last several years, many Catholic educators, school superintendants, and bishops, as well as parents, have questioned whether the current educational and religious situations in America justify the continuing Catholic educational effort.

Times have changed since the middle of the nineteenth century, when the Catholic schools were brought into being on a large scale. In those days, the waves of Catholic immigrants from Ireland, Germany, and later from Italy and Central Europe found that they were frequently unwelcome to the American population. Not only so, but the schools provided for public education were, in many instances, *de facto* Protestant schools. Protestants, after all, were in the majority of the population, and the schools reflected the background and preferences of the parents.

In such a climate, Catholics felt (not always without reason) that the public schools might well provide a threat to the Catholic faith of their children. From this fear grew the development of the Catholic school system in the United States.

What many Catholics are asking now, however, is whether or not this situation has so changed that Catholics cannot be entrusted to public schools without the least danger to their faith. Largely as a result of Catholic effort, the public schools have become "neutral" so far as religious indoctrination or climate is concerned.

Further, Catholics have begun to realize that, at best, Catholic education can only hold the line without advancing it. At no point have more than 50 percent of Catholic elementary and high school students been enrolled in Catholic schools. Given the population explosion here in the United States, even to maintain this proportionate figure will call for resources of trained teachers and fiscal possibilities which the Church simply does not possess. To cite but one case, that of the largest Catholic diocese in the United States, Chicago. Current figures place the Catholic population of Chicago at approximately 2.2 million; by 1985 that figure is expected to reach 3.3 million. Educationally, there will be an increase of 78 percent in the number of children requiring some form of Catholic education. On the high school level alone, this would suggest that one hundred new high schools must be built by 1985 if the Archdiocese of Chicago is to educate the same proportion of the Catholic high school population as it did in 1965.

On the national scale, it is projected that by 1985 approximately 80 percent of the Catholics in the eighteen to twenty-four age bracket will be in non-Catholic colleges and universities, despite the remarkable advances that have been made toward academic excellence by many of the more than two hundred Catholic colleges and universities in the country. Once again, the Catholic college will face the harsh economic realities which confront all of the private colleges and universities in the United States at the present time. It will be a dark day, indeed, for American higher education when private colleges, many of them among the nation's oldest and a number of them basically denominational in their founding, must collapse like straw-built structures before the gales of economic necessity.

No one can really predict the future of Catholic education in the United States on any level from the elementary school to the university. We have been painting the rather unpromising projection of what faces Catholic education by the year 1985. It is encouraging to report that for the years before that date, Catholic education has been concerned with opening windows and developing a truly ecumenical outreach. No matter what may happen to Catholic education by 1985, it has been officially pledged to an education for ecumenism. The performance, as with any educational blueprint, may fall below the plan, but even the plan represents a notable achievement. I quote here from the program prepared by the American Catholic Bishops' Commission on Education for Ecumenism, as presented to the convention of the National Catholic Education Association in 1966.

The Second Vatican Council, most notably in its decree *On Ecumenism,* has summoned every Catholic to help bring about the achievement of Christian Unity. For over fifty years other

Christian Churches have officially been promoting the search for unity. With the Decree on Ecumenism, the Roman Catholic Church has now fully entered into the ecumenical movement, one of the most important religious movements of our century; and has acknowledged that a basis for the practice of ecumenism already exists through a common profession of faith in Christ and through Baptism.

Aware of this need, the Bishop's Commission on Ecumenical Affairs has created a special Committee on Education for Ecumenism charged with the specific mandate of recommending practical ways of deepening and broadening the ecumenical awareness of both the Catholic educator and the Catholic community.

The Committee on Education for Ecumenism understands its task to be ecumenical education of Catholics in the broadest sense. As a consequence it will be concerned, for example, with adult education as well as with that of the child in a Catholic kindergarten; with the Confraternity of Christian Doctrine as well as with the Catholic high school; with the secular campus as well as with the Catholic campus; with the seminary and house of religious formation as well as with parish life.

In line with these concerns, the Committee proposes the following principles as broad guidelines to promote ecumenical awareness and involvement among Catholic educators and students. Later the Committee will bring out a handbook of specific guidelines which will provide detailed suggestions on education for ecumenism.

1. The success of education for ecumenism rests on an awareness that a poverty exists in the Christian community because of our tragic separations. We need each other. Our basic change of heart consists in a deep conviction that we are incomplete as long as division continues. On a more universal level our separation also creates a "poverty" in the world since we deny it our full witness to Christ by our divisions.

2. Ecumenism is fostered by teaching a renewed theology. In elementary and secondary schools this means a biblical, liturgical, and doctrinal catechesis which form a Christian who has a deeper understanding of the Gospel and who is responsive to the needs

of the world. In universities, seminaries, and other institutions of higher education it means a realization that this renewed theology has developed through contact with other traditions and their scholars and must continue to evolve in this way.

3. Ecumenism also demands a knowledge of and respect for the beliefs and practices of other confessions and religions. Educators should prepare themselves to teach these traditions accurately and sympathetically by going to the sources. Where possible, teachers from these other traditions should present this material; this is especially true at secondary and higher levels of education.

4. Ecumenism requires that Catholics become aware of any religious prejudices and negative attitudes they harbor and strive for their elimination. Because these attitudes are often learned in the home, adult education programs for parents should stress this important principle.

5. Ecumenism lives and grows through encounter. Teachers and students will not develop ecumenical attitudes without person-to-person experience in a religious context. Because of the teachers' vital role in ecumenical education, they must seek out such encounters. Furthermore, education should have as an important part of this encounter ecumenical prayer gatherings or ways suggested in the "Interim Guidelines for Prayer in Common and *Communicatio in Sacris* of the Bishops' Commission for Ecumenical Affairs."

6. Education for ecumenism should issue in common witness and service in the world. Young adults should be so formed in love of God and neighbor that they join with people of other traditions to help resolve the many urgent social problems of our day.

7. All these principles must be internalized through mediative prayer for unity which transforms the Catholic making him "eager to maintain the unity of the Spirit in the bond of peace." (Eph. 4:3.). As the Decree on Ecumenism urges, "This change of heart and holiness of life, along with public and private prayer for the unity of Christians, should be regarded as the soul of the whole ecumenical movement, and merits the name, "spiritual ecumenism." Such "spiritual ecumenism" is always faithful to the revelation of our Lord handed on by the Catholic Church.

On the basis of such broad principles, the Committee on Education for Ecumenism hopes, through its work, to hasten among American Catholics the realization of the Second Vatican Council's urgent plea for ". . . all of the Catholic faithful to recognize the signs of the times and to take an active and intelligent part in the work of ecumenism."

We have referred often enough in previous pages to ecumenism to make it clear that the phnomenon is both a welcome fact and, on occasion, a suspicious fad. In order to achieve that unity which was Christ's intent and the proper desire of the ecumenical movement, each of the Christian churches will be called upon to lay aside some of its most cherished characteristics and traditional attitudes. This side of the ecumenical movement formed the basis of a joke making the rounds recently.

Jesus, meeting with an interfaith group, said to them, "Men, I've got an idea."

The Presbyterian answered: "Just a minute. Is it sophisticated?" The Baptist said, "Is it moral?" The Methodist said, "Is it nonalcoholic?" The Disciples of Christ member said, "Is it scriptural?" The Lutheran said, "Is it evangelical? The Quaker said, "Is it quiet?" The Catholic said, "Is it authoritative?" The Episcopalian said, "Is it archaic?" Christ said, "Forget it."

It is always tempting, but dangerous, to go beyond the joke and try to imagine what might have been Christ's "idea." I would not, however, be too surprised if His new idea were not really a very old one: "Feed the hungry, give drink to the thirsty, clothe the naked . . ."

On this aspect of the Christian mandate, the Churches have up until the past dealt only with the coffee spoons of Charity, and not with the bulldozers of justice. The task of the Christian, however, is not merely to minister to the wounds inflicted on individuals by the injustices of society, but also to seek to root out the causes of inequity and injustice, to cure society as well as to comfort its victims.

Only within the last decade have the Christian churches begun to give even a minimal collective response to Christ's all-important imperative to give even the cup of cold water in His name to the least of His brethern. The Second Vatican Council, The World Council of Churches, various national bodies of Christian denominations have now begun to search their hearts and their coffers to meet the growing international demands for justice as well as charity. The American Catholic Bishops, in their Pastoral Letter of November, 1968, had many things to say on these points, but their remarks were drowned out by the clamor and shouting over their earlier-reported remarks on *Humane Vitae* and contraception. Even in their remarks on national and international justice, the American Catholic bishops failed to include an ecumenical sweep to their considerations, and it might not therefore be amiss to conclude this book on American Catholicism with certain questions posed, not to American Catholics alone, but to the entire American Christian community, which will play such a strategic role in the shaping of the future for all mankind.

Alike, we Christians must recognize our pre-ecumenical solidarity with the rest of mankind, with those who have a different faith or no faith, in the accepted ecclesiastical understanding of that term. Before we are Christian, we are human beings and members of the family of God the Father, shaped by His creating hand, called into being by His breath. Wherever we turn in either the Old or the New Testament, we are forced to confront, not an anthropology, but a religious understanding of man's origin and destiny. Since a divine origin and destiny are common to every man, his links to every other man are beyond his forging or his power to break. Regardless of whether those who do not share this Judeo-Christian view of man recognize themselves as sons of God, we recognize them as such. We can only speak of them and to them as our brothers, whose dignity we have neither designed nor given and with whose destiny we are not allowed to tamper.

Alike, the Jew and the Christian believe that in the last sifting of reality there is only one history. This is the record of God's continual breaking-in upon the world of man and speaking to man through event, even as he spoke to Moses through the event of a bush that burned yet was not consumed. No Christian has the right to put man-made limits to God's capacity to speak through events. We can only strive to hear what God may be saying through events, even through the events of this glorious, but torn and often tragic country.

What, for example, is God trying to say to us Christians through this event? We in the white Western community comprise less than one third of the world's people, and yet consume more than 60 percent of the world's goods, and control more than 70 percent of the world's resources.

What do we make of this event? The world has indeed, as we are so often told, shrunk to the dimensions of a village. But in this village, we Christians of the white Western community, *we* live in the houses set upon the hill. We are moated from our fellow villagers by green and spacious lawns, scandalously conspicuous for our expenditure on luxuries and our waste of necessities.

What do we make of this event? That the number of villagers who are nonwhite, non-Christian is increasing rapidly, to the point where by the year 2000, which is not very far away, we will be an even smaller minority than we are at the moment. The world of 2000 will be one wherein the population of China alone may number 1,700,000,000 people, 400,000,000 more than the present population of Europe, North and South America, the Soviet Union, and Africa combined.

Even so brief a glimpse as this into the year 2000 opens our eyes to some of the future tasks of Christian theology if that theology is to be placed at the service of the Word. It makes us aware, for example, that the Christian must confront the fact of poverty. Unless the projections of sociologists, demographers, and economists are completely flimsy and without fact, the world of the year 2000, brown, black, and yellow, Afro-Asiatic, non-Christian, secularized, will also be dominantly a world of the poor. Do we have an acceptable Christian theology of poverty? What, in practical pastoral terms, does it really mean to be a Christian in a world dominantly poor? What does it mean to be a follower of the poor Christ who had not whereon to lay his head when one is himself a citizen of affluence, realizing that approximately 70¢ (seventy cents) out of every tax dollar will be expended directly or indirectly upon armaments.

For war, too, is bred in the offal piles of poverty. Not necessarily wars between nations, but wars within nations. Of the cases of armed strife which have occured since the end of World War II, the overwhelming majority, as you know, have been civil wars, wars of revolution, if you will. Christian theology in the future must deal more seriously than it has for the past two centuries with the question of war—war between nations, and war within nations. The statements on war and peace contained in the Constitution on the Church in the Modern World or in the statements of the World Council of Churches bespeak a Christian passion for peace. They can scarcely be considered, however, to represent a full-bodied Christian theology of either war or peace. Yet obviously, any theology which pretends to be pastoral in the future cannot evade the issue of war and peace. What word will theology place at the service of the Word when theology speaks, not to the cadres of committed Christians, but to the world of men who live (must it be forever?) beneath the dark cloud of terror and violence?

What is God saying to us through these events? Is he not trying to say that we must learn from each other? Must we not teach our children that in the world which they will inherit, they must be the conscious heirs of all that is most authentic in what we call, sometimes too glibly, the Judeo-Christian tradition? We ourselves must attempt to become now, and hope that our children will be in the future, the *anawim,* the "spiritually poor," open constantly to the breathing of the spirit of God. This much, at least, we can hope to do together, if we make the effort to understand who we are and who the other is.

We can attempt to show somehow the emerging world—brown,

black, illiterate, impoverished—that we are indeed their brothers, for each of us holds dear the ancient words of Isaiah: "The Spirit of the Lord is upon me because he has anointed me to bring good news to the poor. He has sent me to proclaim to the captives release and sight to the blind, to set at liberty the oppressed, to proclaim the acceptable year of the Lord and the day of recompense."

To suggest that we, separated Christians who are so divided in creed might yet be united in deed, is of course to suggest a complete reversal of many of our long-held and deeply cherished attitudes and convictions. But this is *kairos,* the acceptable time of the Lord. And even *chronos,* the time measured by calendars and clocks tells us that there is little time left. Can we not speak with one voice against the impalpable injustices within our own society, and move with one heart toward the healing of the wounds of mankind, God's family and ours throughout the world?

It may well be that in order to do this, the churches must strip themselves of many of their possessions and relinquish something of their smug righteousness. We need to show in our actions the compassion of the God in whom our brother does not believe. Visionary? Perhaps. Impossible? Not to the *anawim,* the little one of God who are yet great—an Abraham, a Moses, a Mary of Nazareth, a Francis of Assisi, a John Wesley. Not to the *anawim,* who know that the surest sign of God's power is always man's native incapacity to accomplish God's design. For the *anawim* of our age must come to know what the *anawim* have always known —that only he who can see the invisible can accomplish the impossible.

13

Postscript

Much to my surprise, the tour of the house has ended in the Upper Room. Other guides could have given you a more thorough tour, and could have explained better than I the history of almost every object we have seen. Others could have given reasons why certain objects, which seem anachronistic as a candle mold, are still in use. Any guide would, I suspect, have nonetheless ended with you precisely where I have. This Upper Room has not, frankly, seen too much use for several centuries. The original furniture was kept here, of course, and it was always a place of religious pilgrimage. Indeed, on the feast that we hold sacred to the Holy Spirit, the room could be rather crowded with visitors. Apart from that, there was really rather little effective use made of this room. It was for this reason, perhaps, that when Pope John XXIII decided to open a few windows, the first windows he opened looked out upon the world from this room. Once again, the Holy Spirit manifested Himself in Wind and Fire.

Wind, of course, destroys but also cleanses; fire consumes but also purifies. We have seen some of the dual action of wind and fire as they have moved through the household of the Roman Catholic Church.

The house, as a consequence, has not been tidy, with everything in place; it does not, to put it bluntly, look like we wish our own homes to look when guests are expected or friends drop in. But it yet remains my house, and that of more than half a billion other Christians. We love this house, because it is the place wherein we have met the Triune God and in which He is forever Emmanuel, God with us. It is He, indeed, Who is the Master of the house and it is He Who has called for the rather massive reconstruction whose sights and sounds have confronted you at the opening of every door, the turning on every stairway.

As was to be expected, the tenants frequently disagree over precisely what the Master of the house had in mind. The entire history of the Church seems to show that God makes His wishes known through broad descriptions rather than through detailed blueprints. I cannot, of course, pretend to know whether God wants a closet ripped out in a given room, or merely made bigger, nor can I hope to discern what the interior of the house will look like when, in two years or two centuries, the present renovation will have been completed.

But this much I see, with the eyes of faith which are illumined by what light has been given them, not only by the Second Vatican Council but by the entire history of God's dealings with man through the Christian community founded on the life, death, and resurrection of His Son. The Roman Catholic Church, at the moment, is passing through a time of trial. It is not the first such trial, nor will it be the last. Another way of saying this, and a more meaningful way, is to say that the Roman Catholic Church is carrying its Cross. But in this particular hour, it is carrying the Cross, not alone, but with all the Christian churches who find themselves at a point in history where an old order is dying, and a new world is struggling to be born.

Such, obviously, was the situation in which He carried His Cross—He Who came to make all things new. His death was followed by the triumph of His Resurrection and the coming of the Promised Paraclete. The time is indeed that of a second Pentecost for all of us. The task of the Christian Churches is together to answer the Pentecostal summons. To forsake our fears and jealousies of each other, to leave aside our ecclesiastical vanities, to leave the false security of this Upper Room and to move out together, with a courage not our own, into a world which has never—never yet—*really* had the Gospel preached to it.

"The night is far gone and the day is dawning" (Rom. 13:12). Is there a Christian, in our time, who has not felt, through an open window, the brushing of the Pentecostal Wind upon his cheek, and seen in the fires of sunrise the presence of the Flame?